Sic 'Em Donald!

Dialogue with a Patriot

BJ Melton

AreULost Press
For more information:
info@areulost.org

Cover Art by Jan Inman©

Sic 'em Donald!

What people are saying about, *My America is Back*

5.0 out of 5 stars Many will like it, many will not, but penned by a true Patriot.

March 25, 2018

At 93 years, Mr. Melton has seen his share of politics (good & bad), world issues (war, poverty, disasters, etc.) and still maintains a high level of current event awareness, while adding some personal events, humor, struggles, and religious beliefs he has experienced throughout his life on this earth. He still drives, plays golf, bowls, loves his wife, Clarene, and his Texas Tech Red Raiders. BJ enjoys his grand and great-grand kids and speaks with them often. In general, he enjoys life that his GOD has given him. He is of sound mind and is not afraid (or ashamed) to express his views of the past and current political Scene and truly believes that Mr. Trump has the best interest of all Americans in mind and wants us to return to the great nation that we have seen in the past. His religious beliefs stem from what the BIBLE teaches everyone about right and wrong and he struggles with the morality issues that are overtaking the country today. He doesn't have the answers for immigration, gun control, homosexuality, abortion, terrorism, ISIS, or the many problems that persist today, but he does believe in GOD and Country hoping there are others that share his concerns and that Mr. Trump and the leaders in Washington (both Republicans & Democrats) will bring us back to greatness again!

Larry Denson

5.0 out of 5 stars Great revisit to last presidential election and first few months of Trump's Presidency.

March 9, 2018

Melton writes with humor, wisdom, patriotism, and passion as he covers this brief span of history. His discussion of pertinent events on a sometime daily basis will inform, revive your recollection and bring a smile to your face as you relive the last presidential election. The author is an obvious Trump fan and believes if anyone can restore our country, Trump can.

Kenneth G. Sewell

The author is my father-in-law. One of the superb joys of my life is 36 years of being married to his daughter. He and Nancy did a great job raising her. It is with the same care of a father, grandfather, patriot, engineer, and Navy veteran of World War II that BJ writes and sends his "Thoughts for the Day." This compendium from the summer before the election to Christmas 2018 is poignant, funny, sobering, and laugh out loud. That accurately describes the range of thought and feelings readers will experience.

Jay Inman, US Army, Lieutenant Colonel, Retired, CEO of AreULost Publishing, Author of nine fiction books including *Walking at the Top of the World*

DEDICATION

**This book is dedicated to my son,
Captain Rickey Melton, a Vietnam War hero
who died before his time
January 9, 2018,
Rest in peace, Rick**

Sic 'Em Donald!

ACKNOWLEDGMENTS

All the people who made this book possible.

BJ Melton

FORWARD

We all have thought and opinions.
In this book,
Sic 'Em Donald!, Dialogue with a Patriot,
I am exposing for all to read, my thoughts and opinions from
Aug 2017 to Dec 2018
about our President's first two years in office.
You will see my obvious bias in favor of Donald Trump.
And, hopefully, you will understand the reasons for my bias.
If you agree with me, I will take it as a compliment. If you disagree
with me, Que sera, sera.
Mixed in with the political stuff is a little humor and some of my
personal life, of which I am both proud and thankful.
The Lord has blessed me beyond measure.
Enjoy

Lyrics

The word is about, there's something evolving, Whatever may come,
the world keeps revolving...
They say the next big thing is here,
That the revolution's near,
But to me it seems quite clear
That's it's all just a little bit of history repeating.
The newspapers shout a new style is growing,
But it don't know if it's coming or going,
There is fashion, there is fad
Some is good, some is bad
And the joke rather sad,
That it's all just a little bit of History repeating.
And I've seen it before
And I'll see it again
Yes I've seen it before
Just little bits of history repeating
Some people don't dance, if they don't know who's singing,
Why ask your head, it's your hips that are swinging
Life's for us to enjoy
Woman, man, girl and boy,
Feel the pain, feel the joy
Aside set the little bits of history repeating
Just little bits of history repeating

Sic 'Em Donald!

And I've seen it before
And I'll see it again
Yes I've seen it before
Just little bits of history repeating
'Those who do not learn history are doomed to repeat it.'

America has a glorious history, one of sacrifice, bravery, and a dedication to freedom. Those who have gone before, Patrick Henry, George Washington, Abraham Lincoln, Dwight Eisenhower, and millions who paid the ultimate price for our freedom, are part of our history we must not forget, But we are forgetting!

American history is no longer taught in our schools. Millions of young people have no feeling of pride or patriotism, or realization of what they have inherited. An ideology has developed by many who are determined to destroy all symbols of our history such as statues, our flag, the constitution, historic landmarks, etc.

Worst of all, they are rewriting our history, painting a country that is evil, selfish, and uncompassionate. They are spreading lies about the ideals America was founded on, belief in God, freedom of religion, and individual right to life, liberty, and pursuit of happiness.

My first book "My America is Back" covered the 2016 Election with almost daily thoughts (from June 2015 To August 2017), each page being "a little bit of history', so to speak.

Day-by-day my thoughts pointed to the demise of the country this 93year-old WWII Veteran remembers and expressed the hope President Trump could BRING MY AMERICA BACK!!

MAGA!!!

1 – Get Outta Town

Thought for the day Aug. 9, 2017
Hate groups

The Democrat party is the world's most successful HATE group.

It attracts poor people who hate rich people (but not Democrat rich people), black people who hate white people, gay people who hate straight people, feminists who hate men, environmentalists who hate lifesaving oil and gasoline, bratty college kids who hate their parents. But their real hate success is attracting Journalists who hate Republicans and who work tirelessly trying to convince the rest of us that we should join the hate group and vote Democrat!

SIC 'EM DONALD! MAGA!!!

Thought for the day Aug. 10, 2017
More distorted humor

Trump gave up his billionaire life style to be humiliated, ridiculed, and slandered, to save America.

The 'tolerate' intolerant claim Trump is going to destroy America, so to prove it, they go out and riot, destroy property, burn buildings, steal, march up and down the streets carrying hate signs, and shouting profanity. Then, as they go about destroying America, they say "See, I told you Trump would destroy America." So, it is Trump's fault."

They are as useless and smart as a twisted nail.

SIC 'EM DONALD!!!
MAGA!!!

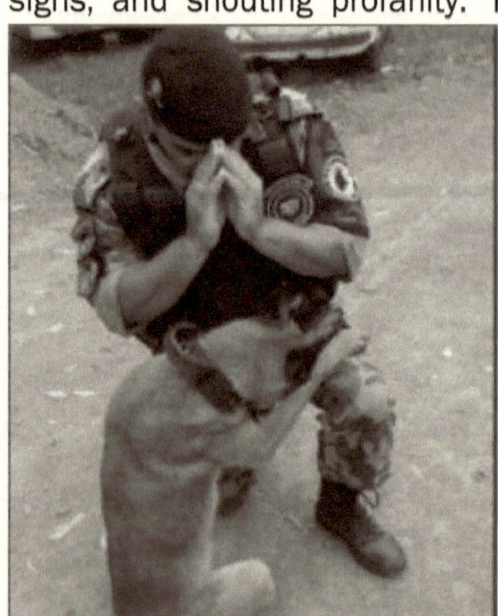

Thought for the day Aug. 11, 2017

If a dog can pray, surely you can, too... Donald and America need lots of prayers.

SIC 'EM DONALD! MAGA!!!

Thought for the day Aug. 12, 2017
Get outta town!

Historically, 'former' Presidents can't get out of Washington soon enough, glad it is over.

What if, then, when we elect a new President, the former President doesn't believe he is a former, but hangs around Washington trying to convince people he is not a former, but is a still is?

Today we have one of those, undermining our American system, and his behavior is rude, uncouth, and dangerous.

Reminds me of the saying

"Do unto others BEFORE they can do unto you."

SIC 'EM DONALD! MAGA!!!

Thought for the day Aug. 13, 2017
He looks like he is smiling.

So, does this dog.
But don't turn your back.
Neither one is your friend.

SIC 'EM DONALD!
MAGA!!!

2 - Hatred

Thought for the day Aug. 12, 2017

HATRED

In 2016 there were 917 hate groups in the United States most of them dedicated to "Dump" Trump.

Saturday, August 12, a peaceful group gathered in Charlottesville, Virginia for a picnic and to promote Making America Great Again.

It seems apparently obvious that Obama shipped in a large group of Neo-Nazis with the intent of crashing the picnic and causing a riot.

Did the peaceful group stand and watch and turn the other cheek when the Fascist starting beating on them? Did they disband, say I am sorry you don't agree with what we are doing?

Did they give up their right to 'peacefully' assemble?

What would you do? Would you fight back?

I hope so. They did!

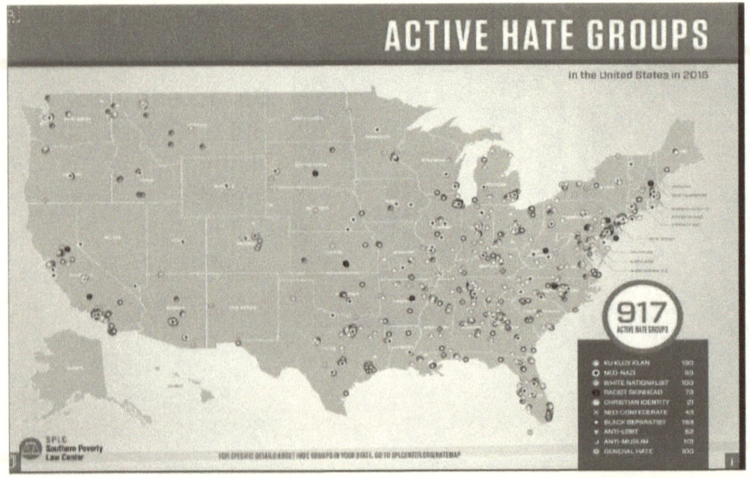

(I am saying this as an outside observer. it is what I think)

The FBI must find those responsible for this terrorist attack, because that is what it is. Who is their leader? Obama?

Who is paying them?

George Soros?

SIC 'EM DONALD! MAGA!!!

Thought for the day Aug. 13, 2017

HATRED

Saturday, President Trump was scorched by the media for not specifically condemning Hate by naming Hate groups. In Dallas 5 policemen were gunned down by one of Obama's Black Lives Matter friends. No comment by Obama. No comment by the media. Besides the Media, and Congressional Democrats, there are hundreds of hate groups in America.

Here is a description of two. BAD!! Neo-Nazi groups share a hatred for Jews and a love for Adolf Hitler and Nazi Germany. While they also hate other minorities, gays and lesbians and even sometimes Christians, they perceive "the Jew" as their cardinal enemy, and trace social problems to a Jewish conspiracy that supposedly controls governments, financial institutions and the media.

Racist Skinheads form a particularly violent element of the white supremacist movement and have often been referred to as the "shock troops" of the hoped-for revolution.

The classic Skinhead look is a shaved head, black Doc Martens boots, jeans with suspenders and an array of typically racist tattoos.

SIC 'EM DONALD! MAGA!!!

Thought for the day Aug. 13, 2017

HATRED

Hate is NOT a many splendored thing.

Have you ever noticed how easy it is to hate something or someone? Have you ever noticed how your love for something, or someone can be turned to hate by a rumor or insignificant event?

Hate has been with us since Cain killed his brother Abel.

But today it seems we have perfected the ability to hate for no reason at all. Last Saturday Trump made a reasoned, sensible, comment about the event in Charlottesville and he was scorched. If he had said nothing until Monday, it would have been the same!

"He did not say what I think he should have said, so I HATE him!"

I remember what Obama commented when

'could have been my son' Trayvon was killed in Florida.

No criticism.

I remember when Obama said 'the Cambridge police acted stupidly' for doing their job.

No criticism.

Then there was Ferguson, Missouri.

When a white police officer shot and killed black robber Michael Brown in Ferguson, Missouri after Brown had robbed a store, assaulted the store owner, assaulted the policeman and resisted arrest, Obama stood behind the criminal Brown.

He even sent three White House representatives to Brown's funeral. No criticism.

Instead of celebrating America's historic progress after voters elected its first black President in 2008, Obama chose to criticize the country and ignited race riots the country had not seen in 40 years since the 1960's.

Hating is so easy. Requires almost no effort.

Thought for the day Aug 18, 2017 To the Dallas News:

Hatred

Your choice of words to make OUR President look bad is disgusting.

Note the highlighted words in your latest BASH!

"Trump returns to 'blame on both sides' view of neo-Nazi clash

After a scripted attempt at damage control over his tepid approach to the violence at a rally of neo-Nazis and white supremacists, President Trump returned Tuesday to the original formulation that drew rebukes from pastors, civil rights leaders and politicians across the spectrum.

While he condemned racists and violence, he also insisted Tuesday afternoon that "trouble makers" on hand to protest the fascists caused much of the trouble in Charlottesville, Va. on Saturday."

As usual everything he said was right, but you and your disgusting Liberal, Socialists friends have such hate and are such vermin, you think you can do anything, say anything, in an effort to Make a Great President look bad.

News for you—it ain't working! Your hateful efforts are generating extreme hatred for you and all the 'Media'!!!

I have to ask, is your hate more sacred, 'privileged' and righteous than the NeoNazis hate?

These hate groups planned this. They poured in from all over. Trump condemned it. You infer he sympathized with them. NUTS! These hate groups are planning more with the help of Your Messiah Obama footing the bill. What will you be doing when the destruction of America is complete?

I wonder-do you have children who will inherit the mess you are helping to make?

SIC 'EM DONALD! MAGA!!!

Thought for the day Aug. 19, 2017
More Hatred

I must be getting old and naive. All week I have been writing about hate, and how it is consuming America. I was thinking some people are hating because of something said or something done.

So, why don't people apologize, say you are sorry, and make the hate go away?

After the W. Va. thing, I saw hatred really get on a roll. So much hatred began to be spewed out by ignorant people, smart people, clergy, politicians, ex-Presidents, and the media, it gave me sick feeling.

Was anybody happy? I asked.

As a matter of fact, there was one group extremely happy- The Southern Poverty Law Center (SPLC).

The SPLC thrives on hate, has a multi-million dollar war chest dedicated to generating hate.

It is a scam that profits from Hate-Mongering. And suckers like "brilliant" Tim Cook, CEO of APPLE just donated $1 million to their slush fund, thinking he did a good deed. SPLC has published a map (which I innocently sent out this week) listing 917 hate groups in America. Many of these are hate groups, but many are decent groups trying to do good. They are only on the list because SPLC put them there, for very selfish reasons.

SPLC was organized in 1971 to divide us and promote hate and they are winning. We are witnessing America's GREAT DIVIDE.

One man, Donald Trump, is trying to MAGA, but the haters are like wild dogs converging on their prey.

He needs our help!

SIC 'EM DONALD! MAGA!!!

Thought for the day Aug. 21, 2017
Racism.
What is racism?
Basically, if you hate someone for any reason, you are a racist!

BJ Melton

Is there a cure for it?
Apparently not.
What we do not seem to realize:
SINCE THE BEGINNING OF RECORDED HISTORY WE HAVE HAD PEOPLE HATING PEOPLE.
So, we have racism today. We will have racism tomorrow.
Think about it.
Some people are happiest when they hate someone.
"It is their right"!
Loving is so hard. Hating is so easy!
The so called 'good' people preach against hate, and at the same time HATE the haters.
"It is their right"!
I think of myself as good people.
But, for one thing, I hate people who slaughter babies.
Racists hate me because God put my soul in a white body.
If I hate them for hating me, I am just as much a racist as they are. Hate is winning because we have professional hate groups promoting Hate for everything. Hate for: Christians, Jews, Blacks, Mexicans, white people, rich people, poor people, young people, old people, atheists, politicians, dictators, police, military, climate control, coal, gas, oil, energy, CEO's, Our President, anybody who does not agree with us, Nazis, Supremacists, hundreds of hate groups.
Should we give up? No! We can't give up.
It is not in the makeup of good people to give up.
We must continue to 'Do good', and trust in GOD!

SIC 'EM DONALD! MAGA!!!

3 – On Being Proud

Thought for the day Aug. 23, 2017

On being proud

Following a speech for the Ages on Monday Night in Virginia, Trump gave a speech for All Americans Last night in Phoenix, Arizona. He called out the media for what it is, The Obstructionist Democrats for what they are, and the hate groups for what they are.

Our President is for us.

Our President has guts!

Our President makes me proud!

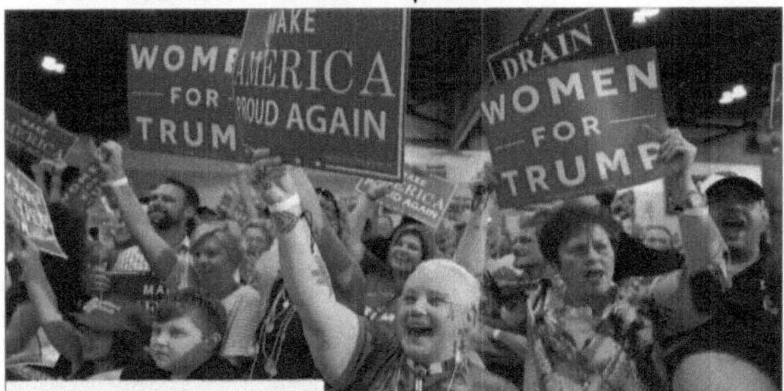

SIC 'EM DONALD! MAGA!!!

Thought for the day Aug. 26, 2017

Why would liberals hate this picture?

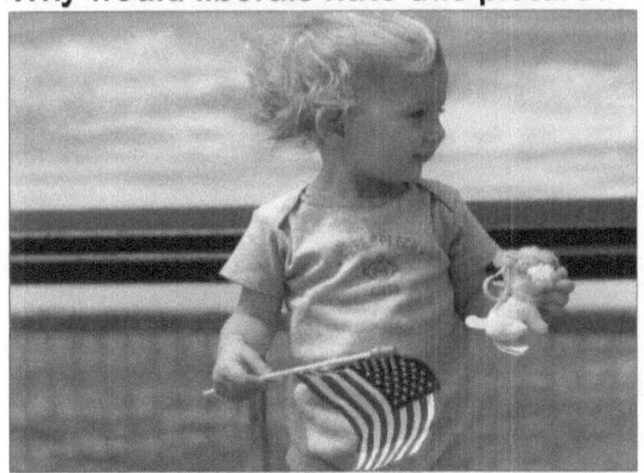

WHY?

Because it represents everything they HATE!!!

SIC 'EM DONALD! MAGA!!!

Thought for the day Aug. 28, 2017

Free Speech?

This weekend at a free speech rally in Berkeley, Ca, attendees were attacked by Obama's masked thugs, using clubs, rocks, and fists. One Trump supporter was attacked by five of the thugs. So brave! Five thugs vs one Trump supporter.

SIC 'EM DONALD! MAGA!!!

4 – The Dallas News

Thought for the day Aug. 29, 2017
The Dallas News, an instrument of hate.

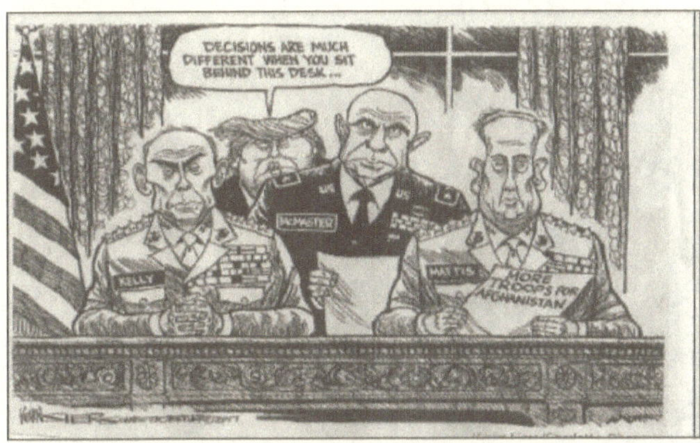

Every day on the " Editorial page" they carry a cartoon such as this depicting Our President in a HATEFUL way.

With their mouths they say, "Love not hate".

With their actions they preach HATE! HATE! This disgusting 'masterpiece' of HATE was on Monday's Op-Ed page.

Borders on treason, but you can't argue with idiots!

SIC 'EM DONALD! MAGA!!!

Thought for the day Aug. 30, 2017
OUR PRESIDENT!

I stand in awe of this man. He has class, pride, dignity, loves the America that was, and means to MAKE AMERICA GREAT AGAIN!

I am in awe of how he can throw off the garbage thrown at him and his family, mostly trite stuff. Yesterday he was faulted for going to Texas TOO SOON?? Melania was faulted for high heels (later changed to sneakers, but not mentioned). Trite stuff! The fault finders are so pitiful.

They grasp at straws. And he has guts!

Faulting him, trying to discourage and divert him from his mission, ain't working. Fortunately, he is always one step ahead. The way he is handling the naysayers is brilliant! He ran for President to MAGA. That is his goal. He will not be deterred, detoured or defeated.

He is awesome! I am proud to call him MY PRESIDENT!

SIC 'EM DONALD! MAGA!!!

Thought for the day Aug. 31, 2017

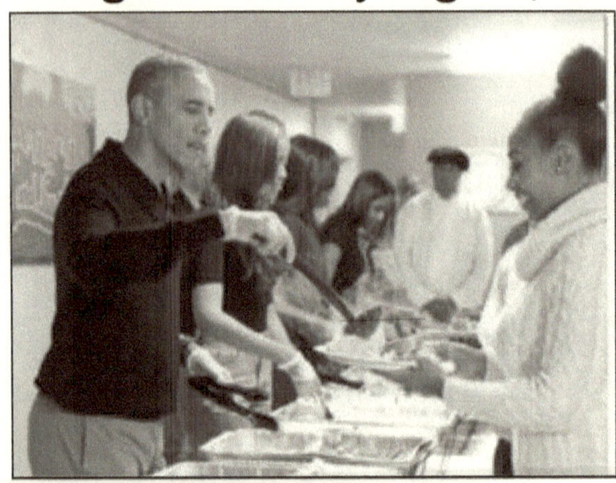

How low will they go??!!

This Twitter went viral AUG. 26 touting Obama in Texas serving flood victims.

In reality, it was a photo op from Thanksgiving Day 2015, and serving veterans. FAKE NEWS IS STILL ALIVE, NOT WELL, BUT ALIVE.

SIC 'EM DONALD! MAGA!!!

5 – Earth Shaking Asinine News

Thought for the day Sept. 21, 2017
Earth shaking asinine news

Melania got on a plane wearing high heels!
   Everybody notices! Disgraceful!

Melania got off the plane to visit the storm area, wearing sneakers.
Nobody notices.
Disgraceful.
All this about "shoes".
Yesterday morning I got up, put on house shoes.
Later I was going to a meeting. Wore dress shoes.
Came home, put on tennis shoes.
Last night I shed tennis shoes for house shoes.
This morning it was house shoes.
   In a little bit I will be wearing golf shoes, because that is most appropriate for playing golf.
   I bet you choose your shoes the same way. Simply asinine.
SIC 'EM DONALD! MAGA!!!

Thought for the Day Sept 2, 2017
Antifa

I thought you might like to see some of Obama's and Soros' friends.
   Makes your heart swell with pride, doesn't it?
   Don't you wish you had friends like this? Maybe have them for dinner? They could entertain you with their experiences, how 4 or 5 sometimes form a team to beat up one innocent individual.

They would be a barrel of laughs, I am sure.

(You might want to run them through the shower before sitting down to dinner)

Thought for the day Sept. 3, 2017

One more thought on THE HEELS! Melania boarded Air Force One in her heels, carrying her own umbrella, with the dignity of a FLOTUS!!!!!

She arrived wearing sneakers, ready to serve as she could, if it would be only to bring attention to much-needed support. Her critics are just a bunch of heels, none of them lifting a finger to help.

Hypocrites!

SIC 'EM DONALD! MAGA!!!

Thought for the day Sept. 4, 2017

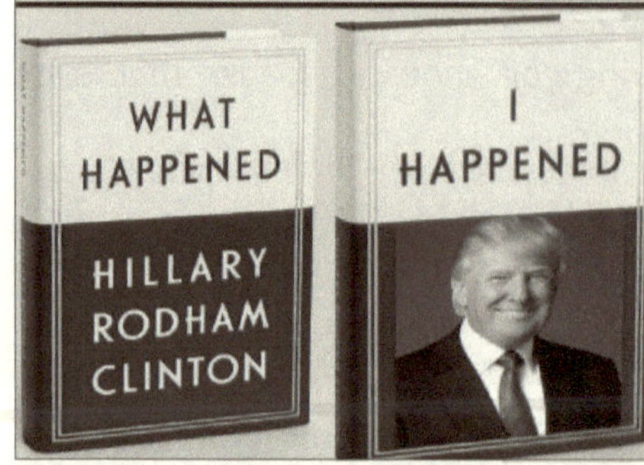

Hillary has a new book going on sale Next week.

The title is "What Happened".

Kinda stupid question seems to me.

Everybody knows what happened.

You don't need the book to find the answer.

Trump happened!

SIC 'EM DONALD! MAGA!!!

Thought for the day Sept. 5, 2017
ISIS destroying history- a 3000 year old statue!

Black hooded"Americans"? destroying

History- a Confederate soldier statue.

Such amazing bravery!!!

Are these 'people' any better than ISIS?

Are these people any different than ISIS?

Where will the stupidity end?

Will Virgin Mary statues be next?

SIC 'EM DONALD!
MAGA!!!

6 – Come Let us Reason Together

Thought for the day Sept. 6, 2017

THIS IS NOT A JOKE, BUT, IF YOU GO TO THE END OF THIS, YOU WILL STILL BE LAUGHING NEXT SUNDAY. IT IS TRUE. I CHECKED IT OUT.

Meet The 'Vogue' Writer Who Criticized the First Lady's Shoes August 30, 2017

Lynn Yaeger, Contributing Fashion Editor at Vogue, criticized the First Lady for wearing stiletto heels before boarding Air Force One to travel to Texas with the President in the wake of Hurricane Harvey.

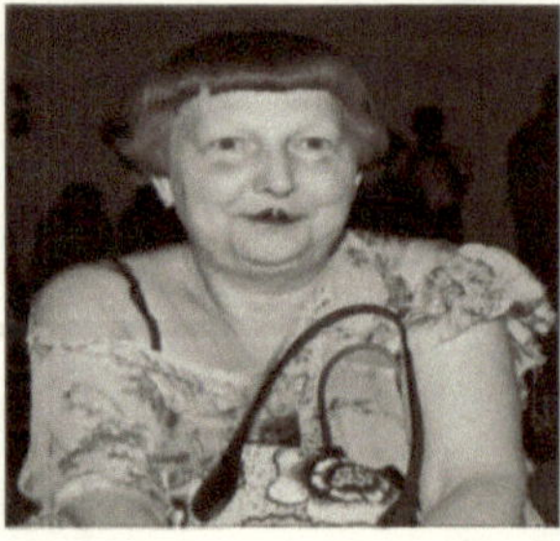

Ms. Yaeger wrote: "This morning, Mrs. Trump boarded Air Force One wearing a pair of towering pointy-toed snakeskin heels better suited to a shopping afternoon on Madison Avenue or a girls' luncheon at La Grenouille."

In her article, Lynn Yaeger remained critical of the First Lady even after she was told by a spokesperson that the First Lady had a change of shoes awaiting her on the plane, when she wrote this: "What kind of message does a fly-in visit from a First Lady in sky-high stilettos send to those suffering the enormous hardship, the devastation of this natural disaster?" When Mrs. Trump did de-plane in Texas, she was photographed wearing sensible sneakers. The pictures on top depicts the First Lady before she boarded Air Force One with the President to visit Texas.

The picture on the right depicts her attire after she and the President arrived in Texas.

<h1 style="text-align:center">Sic 'Em Donald!</h1>

The Vogue Fashion Editor, Lynn Yaeger is pictured to the left (enough said!!!):

<h2 style="text-align:center">SIC 'EM DONALD! MAGA!!!</h2>

Thought for the day Sept. 7, 2017

What a guy! He painted this at a hockey game while the Star-Spangled Banner was being sung!

Patriotism is still alive and well in some places.

SIC 'EM DONALD! MAGA!!!

Thought for the day Sept. 25, 2017

"Come let us reason together"

This morning when I got up, I followed my usual routine, start the coffee pot, get paper in the front yard – but, Whoa! My front door was open. I always close it at night. Well, I am old, so maybe I forgot. I get my paper and a cup of coffee and head for the north bathroom to contemplate things going on in the world.

Suddenly, I hear a baby crying. It is coming from the front bedroom. I look in the bedroom and I am shocked speechless.

There is a man and woman and a newborn baby, born during the night. Turns out they are Mexicans from Honduras, named Juan and Maria, but baby has not been named yet. Then to my surprise, in walks a Mexican boy, about 8 years old, and a girl I guessed to be about 10. I learn they are here illegally, except for the baby. The baby is an American citizen. They have moved into my house and plan to stay. Their clothes, what they have, are already hanging in the closet. Juan asks for towels and soap to bathe, for it has been a long, difficult journey. I am becoming more flabbergasted by the minute. I know I should call the police, but they seem like such nice, well deserving people. And there is the baby. I had to think about the baby, after all, it is an American citizen. While they were bathing, I sat down in my easy chair and began to think.

How did I get in this mess? What should I do? Throw them out in the street? Call the police and have them put in Jail? And there's the baby.

What about the baby? This is really getting complicated!

After they had bathed, they brought me their dirty clothes and asked me to wash them. And they were hungry. Juan said "NO EAT. 5 Days" So, I fried 2 pounds of bacon and scrambled 18 eggs, saying to myself all along "What am I doing? I must be crazy!"

After eating their fill, Juan says "U have nice place. We happy here. Think we stay".

That's it! Juan, you and Maria sit down. Let us reason together. But Juan say "No reason. We like free housing, free food. We stay. Oh, get doctor free medical care for American citizen baby." Then you say this is a fantasy story. It is and it isn't.

This kind of thing has been happening all over America for years. Today we have over 11 million illegals living here, and an estimated 800,000 Dreamers, illegals brought here as children by their illegal parents. They like it here.

They want to stay. Should illegals be returned to their homeland? "Come let us reason together".

SIC 'EM DONALD! MAGA!!!

Thought for the day Sept. 9, 2017

A movie star

September 6, 2017 J Law. a movie star. Oscar-winning actress Jennifer Lawrence suggested the devastating hurricanes in Texas and approaching Florida were signs of "Mother Nature's rage and wrath" at America for electing Donald Trump and not believing in man-made climate change." You have to be in awe of someone, (whose only claim to fame), became rich, memorizing and speaking words. At 27 years old and worth $110 million, she, like so many other actors and actresses, have now acquired, by osmosis, wisdom, knowledge, and an ability to think on their own.

Like I said you have to be in awe.

But not at their brilliance, be in awe of their babbling when they try to think and form words on their own.

SIC 'EM DONALD! MAGA!!!

7 – Lest We Forget

New York City Twin Towers. Sept. 10, 2001

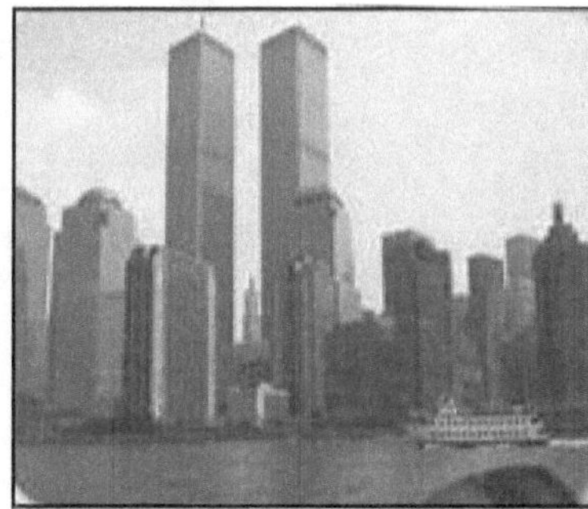

It was a Monday. A cloudy day, with some rain.

A peaceful workday for millions of New Yorkers.
A peaceful day for America.
I played golf.
Donald Trump was in Trump Tower.
It was good to be in America. What could be wrong?

Thought for the day Sept. 11, 2001

Lest we forget. 9.11.2001

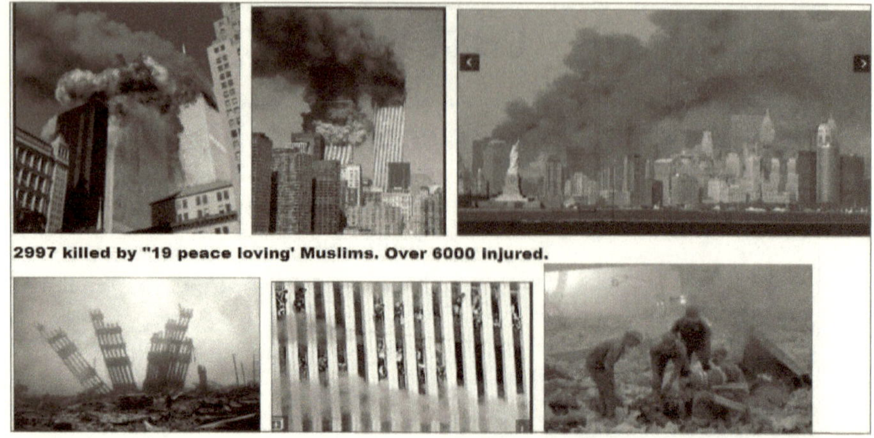

Muslim immigrants. They came to kill Americans. They succeeded. There are more to come. Obama and Hillary said "Welcome!" Where are they?

New York? Chicago? A little town in Michigan? Next door?

SIC 'EM DONALD! MAGA!!!

Bad hurricanes?

Rank	Year	Storm Name	Landfall Wind (kt)	Landfall Pressure (mb)	SS Category
		All Continental U.S. Hurricanes with <= 940 mb pressure at US Landfall			
1	1935	Labor Day	160	892	5
2	1969	Camille	150	900	5
3	2005	Katrina	110	920	3
4	1992	Andrew	145	922	5
5	1886	Indianola	130	925	4
6	1919	Florida Keys	130	927	4
T-7	1928	Lake Okeechobee	125	929	4
T-7	**2017**	**Irma**	**115**	**929**	**4**
T-9	1926	Great Miami	125	930	4
T-9	1960	Donna	125	930	4

Now that hurricanes Irma and Harvey landed on our shores, The Climate Change addicts have begun the chant "Deniers are criminals, want to get us all killed. Punish them!"

My favorite profane expression "Hogwash!"

Of the 10 worst hurricanes on record, 8 (eight) of them occurred before GLOBAL WARMING AND CLIMATE CHANGE WERE INVENTED!

Irma Is tied for 7th. Harvey is # 18.

The sky is not falling.

SIC 'EM DONALD! MAGA!!!

Thought for the day Sept. 15, 2017
A little history lesson

I have BREAKING NEWS for you, all those saints at City Hall, and all those who want to erase American history during the day or in the dead of night:

If you take down every statue on the continent, slavery and the American Civil War will still have happened. If you have minimum wage skills now, taking down statues won't change that. If you're up to your ass in college loan debt, taking down statues won't change that. The nation will still be $20,000,000,000,000 in debt.

We will still be in a global economy. North Korea will still be run by a lunatic who wants you dead. Radical Islamists will still want you dead. People who hate you now, will still hate you, perhaps even more. Soros, Obama and the Clinton's will still be sleazy and corrupt, and you'll still be just a puppet for them.

The Department of Education will still not have educated anyone. There will still be only two genders. Abortion will still be murder. Hillary will still not have won the 2016 election and Bernie will still be a communist charlatan. There will still be opposing views outside your safe spaces. You'll still be accountable for your own choices, and the world will still owe you nothing.

Taking down all the statues will still not change the fact that Communism has been responsible for more slavery and death than the Confederacy ever was. The removal of statues won't change the fact that the first slave owner was a black man. Think about it!

So, if you have a problem with a statue of Robert E. Lee in Charlottesville, Virginia, or in Dallas ,Texas, but no issues with a statue of Communist Vladimir Lenin in Seattle ,Washington , calling you an American would be a lie. I wonder-what are you, really? Oh, and Donald J. Trump is STILL PRESIDENT!

Author Unknown

Thought for the day Sept. 19, 2017

**These are some of Obama's and George Soros'
brave souls rioting, destroying property,
and fighting with police, in St. Louis.
You can tell the brave soldiers by their uniform;
black jackets, face masks, gloves, helmets,
and clubs they carry for 'protection'.**

**This is Obama's war against America and
President Trump. Ever wonder where the 'professional'
made signs come from, and who pays for them?
I repeat THIS IS WAR! It has to be stopped!**

Sic 'em Donald! MAGA!!!

Thought for the day Sept. 20, 2017

I watched and applauded while
President Trump gave his UN speech
yesterday.
Many world leaders praised him.

When I saw Jim Acosta of
Socialist CNN no news
Crying bloody tears,
I knew he had hit a homerun,
not just any home run,

IT WAS A GRAND SLAM!

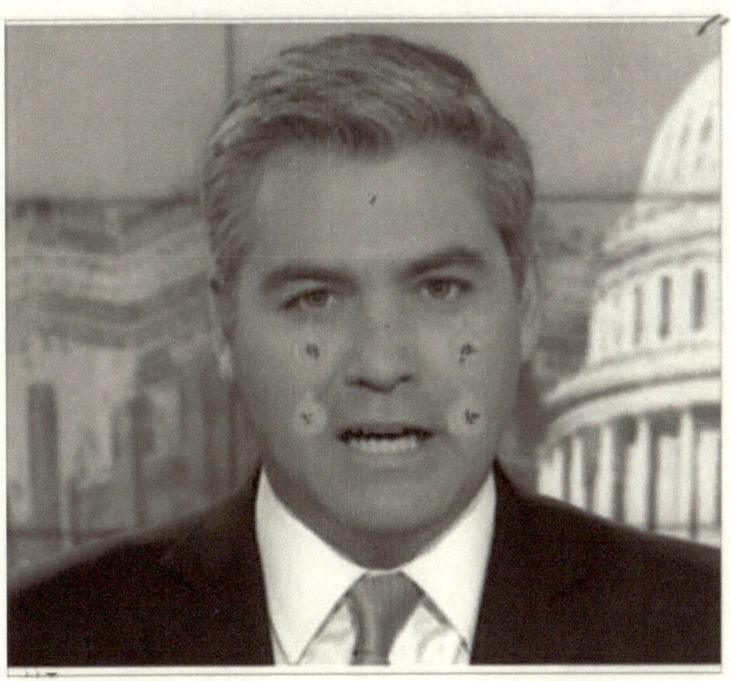

Sic 'em Donald!   MAGA!!!

Thought for the day Sept. 23, 2017
This is a 'snowflake'. Stupid beyond her years.

SIC 'EM DONALD! MAGA!!!

8 – Kneelers

Thought for the day Sept. 24, 2017

On kneeling

Real Americans respect the flag, our National anthem, and America.

NFL football millionaires apparently don't and are biting the hands that feed them.

What is happening?

This picture was taken at the Thursday night game in San Francisco.

♫Empty seats

Oh, keep them coming! ♫

Today the Pittsburgh Steelers stayed in the locker room for the anthem in Chicago.

They lost.

Today, in London, many Baltimore Ravens knelt.

How long can the NFL survive the Fan boycotts?

♫Empty seats

Oh keep them coming♫

Trump was right. Fire the whole bunch!

SIC 'EM DONALD! MAGA!!!

Thought for the day Sept.25, 2017

My Hero

Alejandro Villanueva was the only Steeler to come out for the National Anthem, standing in the tunnel.

The Steeler coach, Tomlin, was greatly disappointed he was not successful in keeping 100% of his players in the locker room.

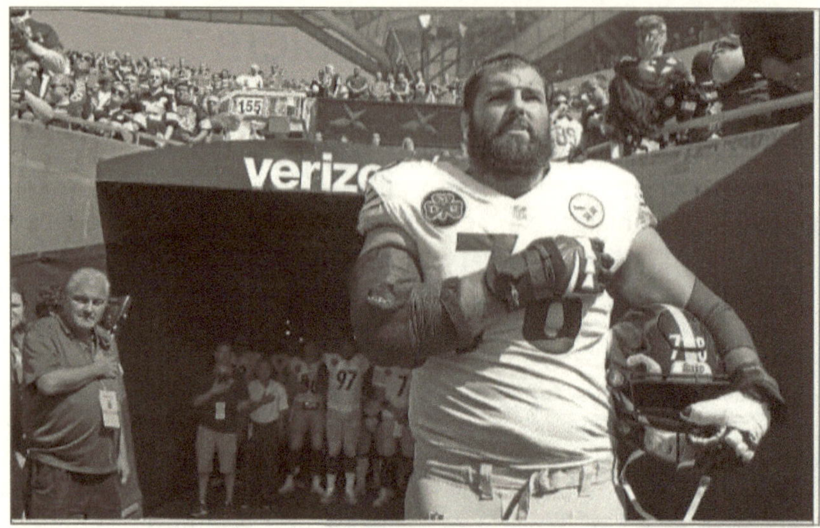

Alejandro Villanueva, an army veteran and patriotic American is A hero in my book! His jersey sales skyrocket, while fans burn other numbers!!

SIC 'EM DONALD! MAGA!!!

Thought for the day Sept. 28, 2017

NFL Cancer

The NFL has a cancer. It was noticed last year when Kaepernick failed to stand for the anthem.

Was the doctor called? No, he was busy chasing down domestic abusers, issuing doses of punishment, and glorying in the power he possesses. It was just one little cell. The cure for the one cell is plainly written in the 'Doctor's' manual. BUT, No big deal.

Left alone, it has behaved like all good cancer cells do, it has multiplied itself.

Now, it is out of control and the cure, if there is one, will be nasty.

SIC 'EM DONALD! MAGA!!!

THOUGHT FOR THE DAY OCT. 8, 2017

WHAT IS YOUR GENDER?

NEW BILL PASSED IN CALIFORNIA;
YOU CAN NOW BE FINED OR JAILED
FOR WRONG GENDER PRONOUN
$1,000 AND/OR 1 YEAR IN JAIL!

It's hard to believe something like this is a real thing. It almost sounds made up but then again, the Left does seem to live in the land of imagination where guns commit crimes, illegal immigrants didn't break the law and boys can be girls.

In the latest move by Ultra Liberal California, you can now face a fine or even go to jail if you refuse to call people by their preferred pronoun.

Now words aren't only scary, they are illegal!

SIC 'EM DONALD!

Thought for the day Oct. 9, 2017

Definition of 'scumbags'

White nationalists return to Charlottesville.

The scumbags are back with their clubs, masks, and profanity. Have you thought about who pays these scumbags to be scumbags?

Obama and George Soros?

White nationalists returned to Charlottesville, Va. on Saturday less than two months after one person was killed and dozens were left injured when violence broke out after the "Unite the Right" rally.

SIC 'EM DONALD!

9 – More Kneelers

Thought for the day Oct. 12, 2017
Kneeling, not praying

To go along with respecting our flag and what it stands for, I think you will find this awesome!

Amazing how he can kneel, thanking others for his ability to make $millions. So grateful!

SIC 'EM DONALD!

Thought for the day Oct. 13, 2017
Disgraceful - HE'S BAAAACK:
OBAMA TO HIT THE CAMPAIGN TRAIL FOR ANTI-TRUMP CANDIDATE NEXT WEEK
October 12, 2017

We knew it would happen eventually, and now it's official.

Even though George W. Bush sat back and truly let Obama do his thing, Obama isn't offering that same courtesy to President Trump.

Scumbag continues his drive to destroy America!

In fact, next week Obama is going to trash Trump on the campaign trail for Democratic gubernatorial nominee Ralph Northam at a rally in Richmond, VA.

Northam used the Obama news to fire up a crowd gathered Wednesday at Richmond's Secco Wine Bar for a women for a Northam happy-hour event. Whoopee! Ick!

Uh, have one on the house from me! Ick!

Thought for the day Oct. 14, 2017

If Hillary had won....

I got to thinking about Slick Harvey Weinstein, Slick Billy Clinton, and no morals Hillary, and I realized my mind was 'slicking' into the gutter.

Then I remembered an adage that says

Actions have reactions which have consequences. Then I thought- if Hillary had won, <u>would we have ever heard about Harvey?</u> Harvey has been running his little playhouse for 2 decades or more. A sex maniac is a sex maniac. A sex maniac with money is no different than a sex maniac with charm. And a woman with no morals, who drags women abused by a sex maniac, through the gutter trying to whitewash her sex maniac husband, is no better than either, and is now lashing out at anything and anyone, trying to salvage what is left of the degenerate liberal Socialist Democratic Party.

Hillary you lost, you deserved to lose. Why don't you go hide and just spend your time counting your filthy lucre.? One other thing, I heard last night Harvey is going for REHAB!!! REHAB? ReeeHab! How do you spell ReHab for an unrepentant Sex Maniac? There are Consequences? Thank goodness Donald won.

SIC 'EM DONALD!

Thought for the day Oct. 15, 2017

Weinstein's money

Do I have to give it back!!??

Sic 'em Donald!

Thought for the day Oct. 16, 2017

In this picture You see Donald Trump, President for nine months, and you see Senate Majority leader Mitch McConnell, a member of the Washington Elite since 1984, (33 years) and a prime reason for term limits.

President Trump is talking. What is McConnell doing?
What is he thinking?   What do his eyes tell you?
What does that smirk on his face tell you?
Think about it.

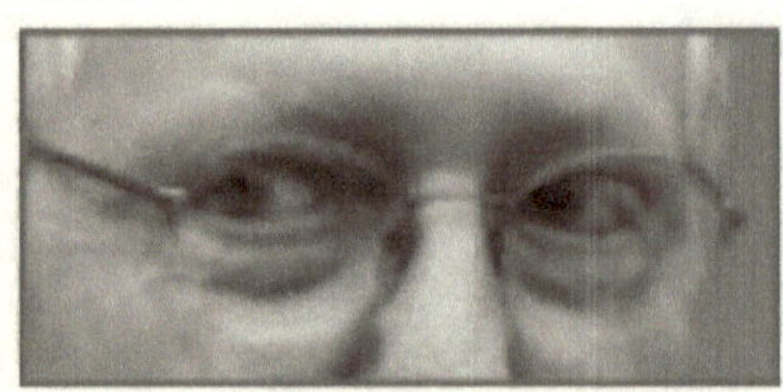

The eyes tell me he is part of the Swamp, he thinks he is better than this upstart. HE IS ACTUALLY LOOKING DOWN ON OUR PRESIDENT.
The 'pursed lips' say "I hate you for messing in my mess kit!"

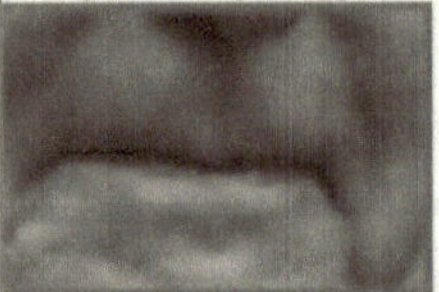

"Pursed lips are a classic sign of anger, including when it is suppressed. It is effectively holding the mouth shut to prevent the person saying what they feel like saying. This may also be an indication of lying or withholding the truth as the person stops themselves from telling the truth."

Sic 'em Donald!

10 – Lips

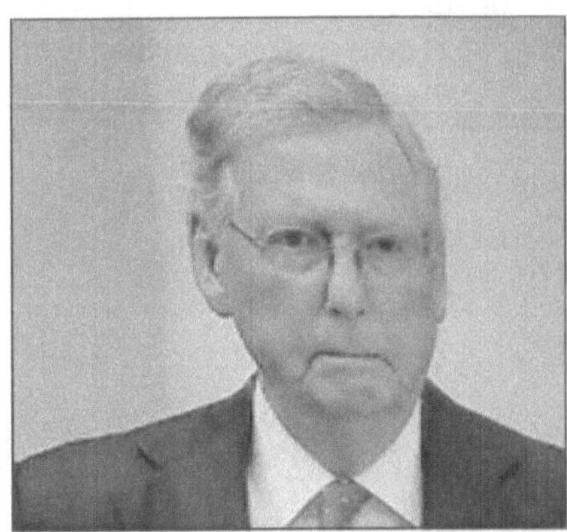

Thought for the day
Oct. 17, 2017
The lips talk

AFTER ONE-ON-ONE MEETING WITH TRUMP, TURNED DOWN LIPS INDICATE MISERY AND/OR UNHAPPINESS.

SIC 'EM DONALD!

Thought for the day Oct 19, 2017
Another enigma

When I hear these people talk:
Obama
The Clintons
Paul Ryan
Mitch McCullough
Schumer
Boxer Graham
Maxine Waters
Pelosi
Others...

I know they are lying, bold-faced. Naive little me will never understand what it is about POLITICAL jobs, any of them: president, senator, representative, governor, mayor, city councilman, or a political appointee, that makes them sacrifice all self-respect for themselves. Is it greed, power, filthy lucre? Some, I know, just become lazy, live the good life on taxpayer money, and repeat their BlueSky promises to the people they are supposed to help.

President Trump is FOR me, I know.

Why else would a man with a brilliant mind, and billions of dollars be willing to put up with the crap the ingrained swamp critters keep throwing at him, day after day?

Then ask yourself, why would these swamp critters keep fighting against everything that would make life better for you and me? I'll tell you why. You have heard about the plantation for black people, Haven't you? I got news for you-we are all on the plantation, servants of our greedy Washington establishment swamp critters.

Look at yourself. The thousands of rules they have made that you have to play by, the iron-fisted IRS that makes you pay taxes through the nose, or they come get you and everything you own. If Trump is unsuccessful in getting us off the plantation, you can rest assured your children and grandchildren will be picking cotton <u>just like you are</u>.

SIC 'EM DONALD! MAGA!!!

Thought for the day Oct 20, 2017
BUSH turned RINO

I am normally a mild-mannered Milquetoast kind of a guy. I like peace and tranquility, sunshine, laughter, good food and REAL friends.

But liars, rabble rousers, con men and women, hypocrites, and naysayers about my America, change my personality.

Yesterday my peace and tranquility were severely disturbed. Ex-President George Bush, famous for saying dumb little things when he was President, <u>infamous for turning mute while Obama was destroying America,</u> has now come out of hiding to express sharp criticism of our current President without naming names. So now he, Clinton, and Obama are bedmates, snorting the same degenerate songs about our President. What are you, George, Really? Disgusting!

Now comes 74-year-old Frederica Wilson, a member of the House of Reps to bad mouth Trump over his "supposed" words to a grieving widow. She made an outright fool of herself, trying to politicize her pretended grief for the death of a hero and for his grieving widow.

Hypocrite. Since 2011 she has voted AGAINST 9 (nine) bills designed to benefit service personnel, veterans, and family members.

REALLY LOVES OUR SERVICE PEOPLE! Ha!
Disgusting!

SIC 'EM DONALD!

Thought for the Day Oct 21 2017
Fooled twice!

Bush "Let's be friends Obama"
"Sure, George, sure."

The Republican Party changed during and after Bush's term in office. Not only did Bush destroy the Republican majority with the Iraq War, he, also, planted the

seeds for Obama's deficits with his own massive deficit spending. Bush paved the way to the Socialist rat hole, and Obama jumped right in, deliriously giggling for 8 dismal years.

President Bush's immigration program was to give amnesty to all the Mexicans so that they can work here, and vote Democrat. What a GIFT!!

Republicans, in general, were a disaster from 2006 to 2008. Bush did nothing.

Congress caved to the Democrats. Bush was supposed to be its leader.

Preserving Republican strength was his responsibility,

He disappeared for long stretches of time after he was re-elected.

Maybe he just got tired of it all. Maybe the weight of his Iraq War was too much to bear.

His second term was all downhill. Then the Party put up John McCain as a sacrificial lamb to run against Obama, just simply throwing in the towel. Another GIFT! I voted for Bush twice. I bragged on him. I liked him. BUT I didn't know him.

'Gentle' George, Sr., '41, his father, made a serious mistake and the Democrats sold him, and us, down the river, depriving him of a second term and giving us sex maniac Clinton for eight years.

I thought George was different.

HOW WRONG CAN A PERSON BE! HE SOLD US DOWN THE RIVER AND GAVE US 8 YEARS OF OMAMA!

Like father like son, I guess.

So being the gracious man that he is, he went away for 8 years, turned stone deaf and mute, while Obama pushed us further down the Socialist rathole. It was courtesy to the new President, he said.

But now, he has joined his friend Obama trying to cut my President in little pieces, and at the same time, tell me and my millions of deplorable friends how stupid we are. And Bush is the same person that said

"Islam is a religion of peace, hijacked by a tiny minority of extremists"!

George Bush, I don't like you anymore. Go back to your rathole and shut up!

SIC 'EM DONALD!

Thought for the day Oct. 23, 2017
The JOY of inflation!

In 1987 I retired with my Social Security and retirement pension.

I was not rich, but comfortable. Life was good. Lately, I have found it necessary to squeeze every dollar, because my outgo started to be more than my income.

For years I went to the grocery store without a list and just bought everything that caught my fancy. Not so now. Yesterday I made a list of 'essentials', went to the store and ONLY bought what was on the list.

I have not bought a dress shirt in years.

Last week I got to thinking I might buy a new shirt, but quickly fell in love with the ones I have.

Why? The cheapest ones I could find were 3 for $120.

I remember buying nice shirts for $9.98.

Wut's happening? I said.

I then checked on what "inflation" is doing to all of us.

Surprise! $100 in 1987 is worth $46 today. I have not had a raise since retiring and my income now will buy less than half of what it would buy in 1987. I have a 2003 Lincoln Town car, paid for, and drives and rides like dream. Clarene has a 2012 Kia Forte, paid for, and gets

35mpg. Obviously, I am not in the market for any kind of car. My house cost $34, 000 to build, taxes and Insurance were a few hundred dollars. Today THEY say my house is worth $350,000, taxes and insurance are over $5000. I am a poor little 'rich' guy.

Inflation is cruel to old folks.

DONALD!! CUT OUR TAXES!!!

Thought for the day Oct. 22, 2017
Doing something good

Last night in College Station, Texas all five living ex-Presidents gathered for a fundraiser for victims of recent hurricanes. What they did was a good thing, I give them credit.

But me being me, I had to ask
"As President, what did they do to make America better?"
The answer was "Nothing!"
As President, Jimmy Carter was probably the ineptest, just ahead of Obama.
But as an ex-President he has done wonders through his Habitat for Humanity.
Thousands of families have been helped, and at 93 years old is still going strong. In the picture you see Clinton, who just could not help himself, taking a last minute jab at President Trump, who spoke by video.

SIC 'EM DONALD!

Thought for the day Oct. 30, 2017
Crooks

I read the paper. I watch TV. I check the internet. I see crooks threatening crooks, trying to prove one crook is more crooked than the other. I, logically, (and I am logical) have to conclude as Forest Gump said:
"Crooked is as crooked does".
It seems like the crooks are everywhere.
Then I wonder, are there no Saints some place? Then I realize, YES! NFL the Saints are in New Orleans, Of course!

11 – Thanks, Obama

Thought for the day Nov. 44, 2017

Thanks, Obama.

One of your friends, Sayfullo Saipov, showed up in New York yesterday driving a rented pickup truck. Suddenly. he saw a bunch of infidels walking and riding bicycles. Allah said "Sic 'em" so he mowed them down, killing at least 8 and injuring 15-20.

"Good job" said Allah.

After running down helpless bicycle riders from behind, he left their mangled bodies scattered all over, and ran into a school bus full of little children. His truck destroyed, he jumped out of the truck shouting

"Allahu Akbar," Arabic for "God is great," Thanks, Obama.

How many more of your "friends" were in included in the millions of immigrants you gave green cards to, in the last 8 years? Where are they? When, not IF, will they show their allegiance to Allah, and mow down some more infidels?

The police shot Sayfullo in the butt. Now we have to clean him up, save him for an expensive trial, and watch some bleeding heart liberal lawyer defend his "rights". Too bad. We would all be better off if the police had just expedited his trip to be with his allotted 70 VIRGINS!

Thanks, Obama. Makes you proud, doesn't it?

SIC 'EM DONALD! CLEAN HOUSE!!!

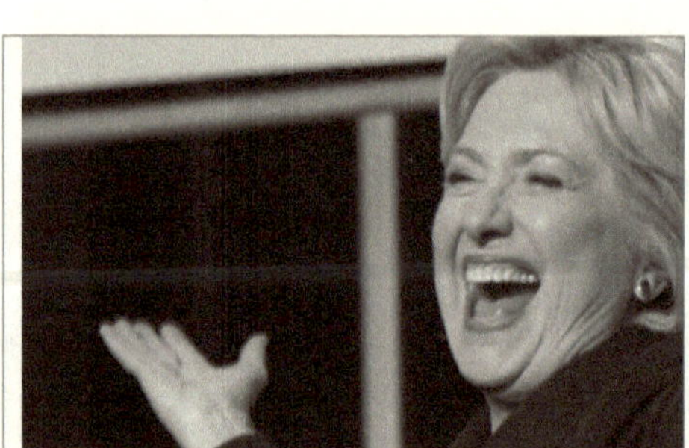

IT'S OFFICIAL: LOOK HOW MUCH HILLARY PAID FOR THE FAKE RUSSIA DOSSIER ON TRUMP...

November 1, 2017   Clayton

After the Russia Dossier story broke loose just over 10 days ago, we learned more and more about just how involved Crooked Hillary was in the production of the Fake Russia Dossier against Trump.

Thought for the day Nov. 44, 2017

The Dossier

$1.02 MILLION.

"It was just for fun"

SIC 'EM DONALD!

Disgusting people

Recently, Chuck "The Clown" Schumer gave a heart-rending talk before a small audience consisting of immigrants, parents of immigrants, grandparents of immigrants, children of immigrants, and grandchildren of immigrants.

It a program by our government that says once an immigrant is on

US soil, they can send back home for the rest of his family, plus anyone remotely kin to the immigrant.

Schumer 'appeared' to shed a tear, vowing to save all such immigrants from deportation.

He is their 'friend'.

Recently, one of his 'friends' rented a pickup truck, drove it into a crowd of walking people and bicycle riders in New York City, killing 8 innocent people and seriously injuring 12-15 more.

What did the immigrant say?

"I wish I had killed more!"

I wonder if Schumer shed a tear for the victims.

Some people are disgusting to the core.

Schumer is one such person.

SIC 'EM DONALD!

I GUESS THIS IS ME!

HAVE A NICE DAY! REALLY!!!

Politics today. Think about it. People treat President Trump like crap, then get offended when he treats them the same way!

SIC 'EM DONALD!

What is a 'suspect'?

This is dumbfounding. The whitewashing of this Terrorist who killed 8 people in cold blood and injured 12 more has begun.

The obvious is obvious, but he is now referred to as a terror SUSPECT, NOT THE KILLER HE IS. He has a family, is a good neighbor, worked hard, his mother visited recently, saw no signs being "radicalized",

Had expressed a desire to return he his homeland.

He also, in a moment of 'weakness', said he wished he had killed more!!!! President Trump is being criticized for saying what

most of us are saying. Now the coldblooded killer is the victim, those killed and injured are just sacrificial lambs.

CNN News headline!

NY terror <u>suspect</u> planned to return to Uzbekistan, sister says.

A woman brings flowers for the makeshift memorial for victims of

Tuesday's terrorist attack along a bike path in lower Manhattan on November 3, 2017 in New York City. Eight people were...slaughtered. The younger sister of Sayfullo Saipov, the man ~~suspected~~ who carried out this week's terror attack in New York, said he had recently expressed his desire to return to his native Uzbekistan.

Ha Ha!

SIC 'EM DONALD!!!

Thought for the day Nov.6, 2017
What is a criminal?

A criminal is someone who breaks the law.

What kinds of laws are there?

Well, the most common kinds of laws are the international law,

Constitutional and Administrative law, Criminal Law, Contract law, Tort Law, Property law, Labor laws, and many others.

Punishment varies for type of violation.

There are fines, financial rewards, jail, prison, death. There are so many laws that we probably break some ignorantly, which is not an excuse.

Almost everybody knows it is against the law to kill another person.

But it happens and for various reasons.

Been happening since Cain killed Able.

There are many different ways to kill someone-MANY!

Guns are one way.

So, Congress needs to pass a law to make it against the law to kill someone with a gun.

But wait! Been there, done that many times already.

Has not worked.

Maybe we could pass a law that says if you are nuts, or just crazy, or angry, or jealous, or just have an urge to kill someone, you can't have gun. That is a great idea.

Now if we could just determine who these people are- Problem solved.

SIC 'EM DONALD!

Thought for the day Nov. 8, 2017

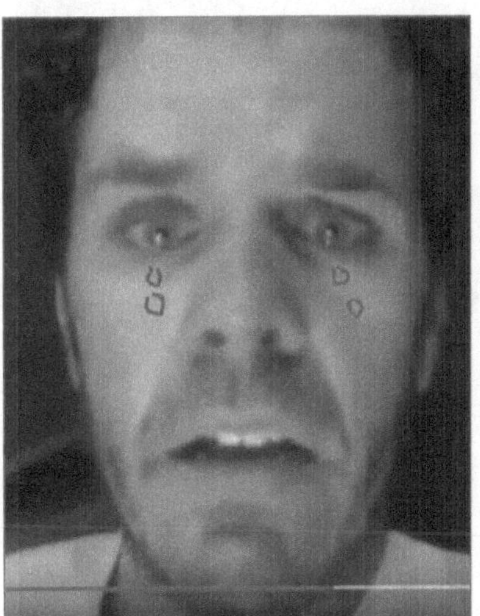

Crying time
2:30 AM Nov. 9, 2016
Hillary concedes! Oh! No!!
Anyone but Trump!

What a blessed day!

SIC'EM DONALD!

12 – Dinner with a Close Friend

Thought for the day Nov. 9, 2017

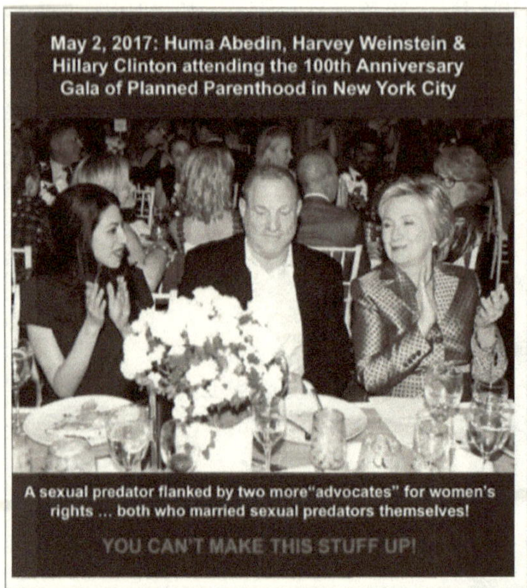

Happiness is Dinner with a close friend!!
What's that old saying "Birds of a feather............." And she thought she 'deserved' to be President. Just one reason the Country's morals have been degenerating,
   SIC 'EM DONALD!

Thought for the day Nov. 10, 2017

On November 10, 2016 the Socialist left, viewed Trump's win as just this-- a horrible, horrible mistake!

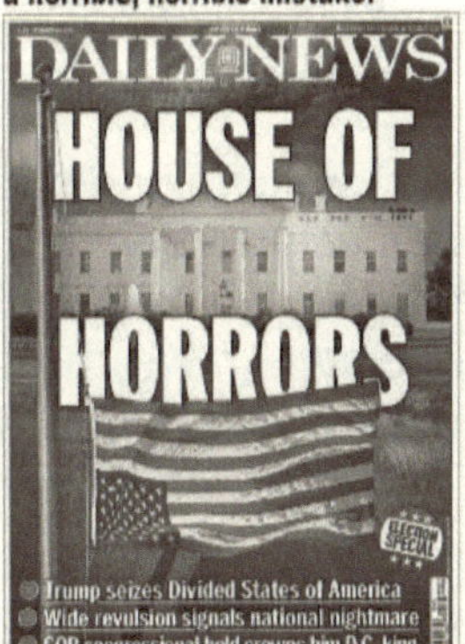

While the Trumpsters viewed his win as a big win for America and rejoiced!

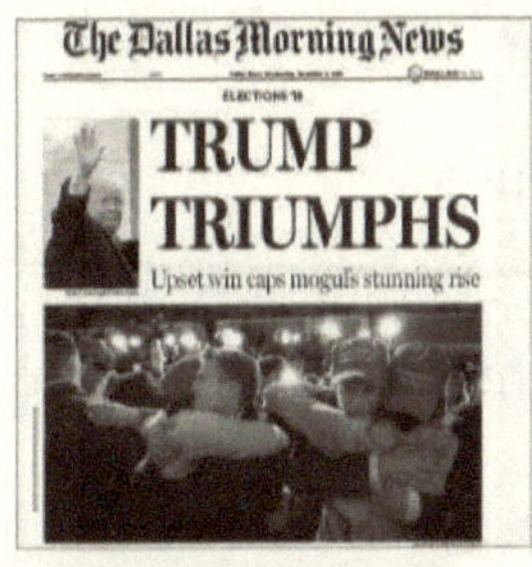

Sic' em Donald!

Thought for the day Nov. 11, 2017
The hanging!
By the Washington Post
Judge Roy Moore---Please stay with me -

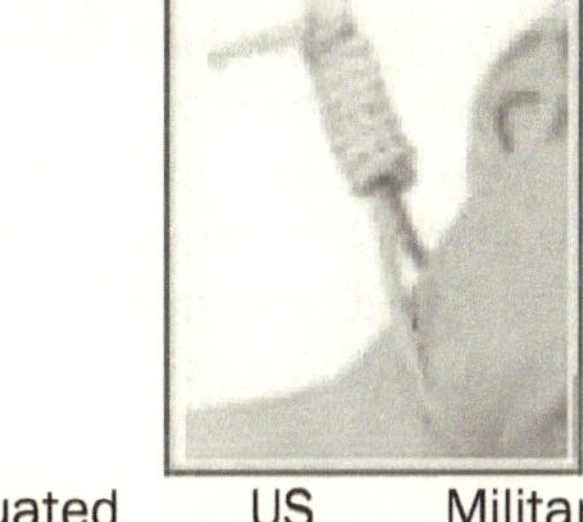

Graduated US Military Academy, served in Vietnam Retired as Captain after 5 years. Is a strong far-right Christian.

Elected 2001 to Chief Justice Alabama Supreme Court

Had monument of 10 commandments installed in judicial bldg.

Removed from office in 2003 for refusing to remove monument.

Elected Chief Justice in 2013.Suspended 2016 for directing Probate judges to enforce State's ban on same-sex marriage.

Is now Republican candidate for Senator, election Dec.12.

UNTIL NOW NO ONE HAS VOICED ANY OPPOSITION TO HIM. The Washington Post, <u>a sworn enemy of President Trump,</u> has now uncovered 4 women who claims Moore molested them.

The prime one, now 54, said she was 14 at the time. Been quiet for 40 years.

Why now?

Let us compare Washington post beliefs with Roy Moore

<u>Washington Post</u>	<u>Roy Moore</u>
Pro homosexual	Anti-homosexual
Pro Muslim	anti Muslim
Pro same sex marriage	against same sex marriage

Anti-Christian   Strong Christian
Socialist-far left, anti-Trump   Far right, Trump supporter
Denies Obama a Muslim   Obama said he is Muslim
Elect Democrat   Must win-Repub. keep one vote margin-Senate
Rino McConnell fears Moore   Moore will fortify Conservative Senate

A victory for the Democrat will stop the wheels of progress dead in its tracks.

And the Washington Post will gloat in its victory for Socialist Communism. Finally, you have to wonder how much did the Post pay these women to bare their souls after 40 years? Money and greed can work wonders on "Recall". 40 years is like yesterday. I recall the day I was born and how excited I was to be here. When I was 8 days old, I had no name, and I asked my mother WHY? She didn't answer. Didn't believe I could talk.

SIC 'EM DONALD!

Thought for the day Nov. 12, 2017
PAIN IN THE BACK

Today is not a good day. My back always hurts when I get up each morning.

I have thought about buying some of the creme advertised for pain relief. Blue Emu is one, and there are many others. I assume most over-the-counter cremes are safe------BUT

Thinking logically, I don't understand how rubbing a creme on my aching back could do anything for pain.

Then this morning, I read about a multi-million dollar fraud scheme by doctors, pharmacists, and marketers.

Special drugs, usually pretty cheap, are written into a prescription. The pharmacist then compounds the prescribed drugs to make a new drug and sells it to the "pain" customer for thousands of dollars.

One pharmacist bragged about making a $1,000,000 a DAY!!

So, why am I writing this?

The paper tells the story of a 22 year lady who rubbed one of these prescription cremes on her back. She said it felt funny and decided to wash it off. One hour later, she was found dead in the bathtub. It is a mystery to me how a creme rubbed on your skin can be absorbed into the body and bloodstream.

I now have to realize it does, whether I understand it or not.

I now wonder about polybacitracin, cortisone, and good old Ben-Gay. MY CONCLUSION: Greed, fraud, lying, and stealing are not limited to JUST POLITICIANS!

Thought for the day Nov. 14, 2017
How to get rich

This morning I watched and listened to Jess Sessions' interrogation by the house Judiciary Committee. The questions, mannerisms, and downright rudeness reminded me of a house full of monkeys. The average IQ has to be between 50 and 100. It is really disturbing to me when I realize they pass laws that control what we can do, or must do, to stay out of jail.

They pick our pockets with tax laws.

They exempt themselves from laws they don't like.

They are overpaid with many Perks.

Left in office 10 years or more they become millionaires.

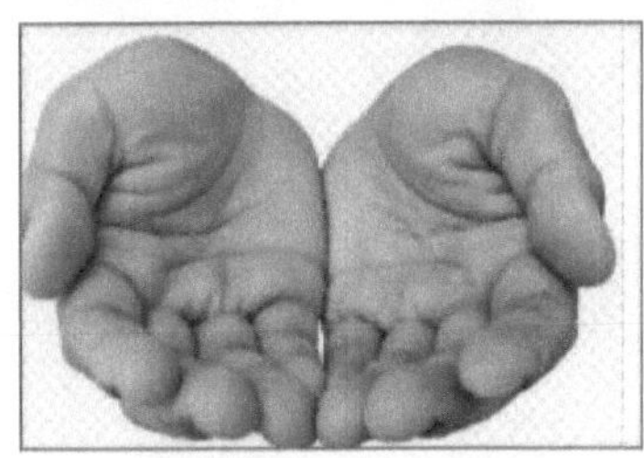

And every lobbyist is greeted with

SIC 'EM DONALD!

Thought for the day Nov. 15, 2017
Harassment!
POLITICS

11/14/2017 03:46 pm ET Updated 18 hours ago

Paul Ryan Announces U.S. House Will Mandate Sexual Harassment Training!!

"Our goal is not only to raise awareness, but also make abundantly clear that harassment in any form has no place in this institution."

Lighting strikes

I am trying to understand this. Congress is made up of adult men and women, and a few who don't know which bathroom to use.

They have all sinned, some more than others.

Some learned from their mistakes. Some learned nothing.

Today they point their finger at the sinner Roy Moore and proclaim "You are BAD, really bad! We don't like you!" All of them now must go to school.

Question: Where will they find a Jesus to teach the course?

I am at a loss for more words.

HYPOCRISY IS IN FULL BLOOM IN AMERICA!

SIC 'EM DONALD!

Thought for the day Nov. 16, 2017
Harassment 'SHUSH' fund

Where did the $15 million go?

Did you know:

Congress has, for many years, appropriated money to itself, to spend for "whatever".

Money appropriated, but not spent, is NOT returned to treasury.

Thus, a shush fund of over a BILLION dollars has been created.

Expenditures are secret and unaudited.

In truth, there is almost no way, for those outside a very select group in Congress, to know how congressional funds are used. That, itself, is scandal enough. The rollover of undesignated funding, coupled with the absence of independent auditing, presents a situation ripe for abuse, AND ABUSE WE HAVE!

All information regarding the funding of Congress should be available to Americans. But, conveniently, Congress exempts itself from the Freedom of Information Act (FOIA).

However, we have now learned that the 'Holier than thou" Congress has, in recent years, SECRETLY paid out over $15,000,000 for

Sic 'Em Donald!

Harassment Charges against Members of Congress by Congressional Staffers.

Now the big question:

WHO WERE THESE PLAYBOYS, OR GIRLS, WHO GOT THEIR BUTTS COVERED WITH TAXPAYER MONEY?

Hollywood is bad, but at least, we know many members of the cast!

But for Congress, not even the SHADOW knows the players.

(You do remember the Shadow on radio, don't you?)

SIC 'EM DONALD! DRAIN THE SWAMP!

PS: And Roy Moore, as bad as he may have been, is not good enough to associate with them!!??

Thought for the day Nov. 17, 2017

Here is a pile of rocks.

Here are some 'angels' in Congress.

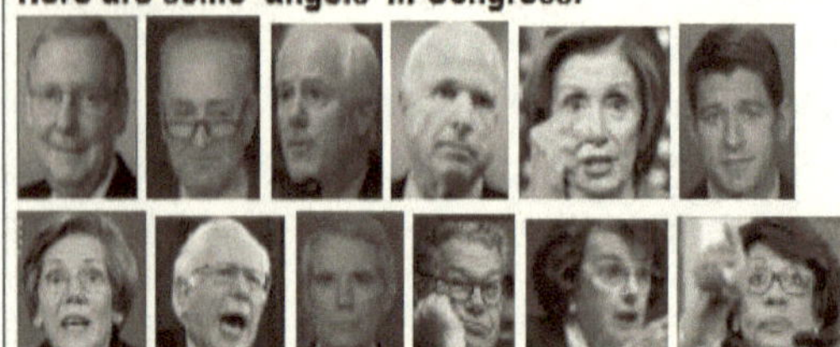

These 'angels' are good at throwing rocks.

But not at each other.

Mainly their target is Trump.

Lately, the 'angels' have added targets, Old Hollywood Weinstein for one.

Now the 'angels' are throwing a shutout at Judge Roy Moore.

Is he guilty or innocent?

We don't know at this point, but he has been found guilty without a trial,

and the rocks are flying.

But not at each other.

They have the BILLION DOLLAR shush fund to cover their

sinful butts!

Uk OH!!! they just caught 'Angel' Senator Franken.

Looks like he may have broken a wing.

I guess the Democrats will ask him to resign, don't you think?

It will be interesting to see if they throw any rocks.

Probably have an 'Ethics' probe and 'whitewash' him.

Sic 'em Donald! MAGA!!!

Thought for the day Nov. 18, 2017

As-sine - Democrat statements:

"You don't need God anymore; you have us Democrats." ~Nancy Pelosi
(Quoted 2006)

"Bill is the greatest husband and father I know.

Sic 'Em Donald!

No one is more faithful, true, and honest than he is." ~Hillary Rodham Clinton (Quoted1998)

And the most ridiculous gem of wisdom, from the "Mother Superior Moron":

"We just have to pass the Healthcare Bill to see what's in it."

~Nancy Pelosi (Quoted 2010)

(As one Doctor said: "That is also the perfect definition of a stool sample."

1st prize

"My fear is if North Korea nukes us,

Trump gonna get us into a war." ~ Maxine Waters........2017

SIC 'EM DONALD!

Thought for the day Nov. 20, 2017
Things are going crazy.

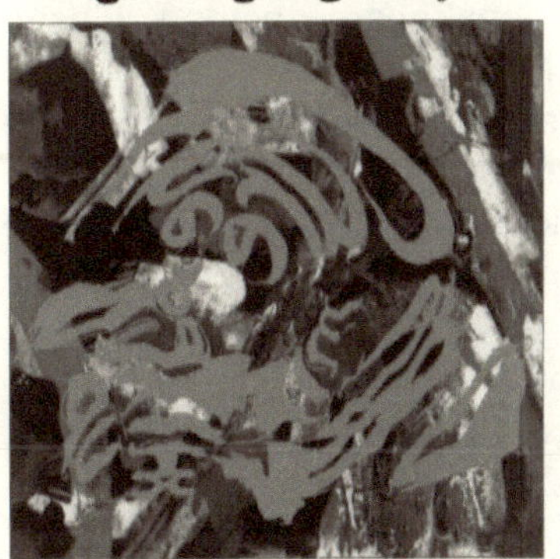

We got Roy and Franken, Tax cuts, Obamacare, Russia meddling, Clinton's lying, harassing in Congress, North Korea nut, Maxine Waters "Impeach 45",

Twitter, Twitter, Twitter, Congress' SHUSH fund, abused women by the score, terrorists, ISIS, home grown killers, anti-gun, pro-gun,

illegal immigrants, legal immigrants, THE WALL, sanctuary cities, poverty, TRADE, NAFTA, trillion-dollar debt, China, Mexico, NATO, Iran, Iraq, Senate leaders,

House leaders, RINOS, Democrats

I AM ALL MIXED UP!

HELP ME, DONALD!

13 - Thanksgiving

Thought for the day Nov. 22, 2017

Thanksgiving

Tomorrow has been pre-determined to be a Day of Thanksgiving. I don't know who decided it, but history told me there was a day back in the 1600s when the Pilgrims had a Thanksgiving Day to celebrate the fact that the Indians did not kill them. To show their gratitude for being alive, they eventually stole their land, killed their turkeys, slaughtered the buffalo, and corralled them on Reservations. The Government promised to take care of them forever, and right there, all of us should have learned what Government promises are worth!

But we learned nuthin.

The Social Security Trust Fund was to be untouchable by the Government, UNTIL IS WASN'T. President Johnson's War on Poverty was supposed to eliminate poverty. What did it do?

It guaranteed a place on the Reservation for millions.

Obamacare was to be a panacea for healthcare. Instead, it just put more naive souls on the Government Reservation.

Today, at least 50,000,000 American souls are on the Government Reservation, and the number is growing every day.

So, what do I have to be truly thankful for? I am going to meditate on that today and see what revelations I have by tomorrow. See you then.

Thought for the day, Nov 23, 2017

If you are warm, healthy, have food to eat, hot and cold running water, indoor plumbing, loved ones nearby, shoes on your feet, a bed to sleep in, money in your pocket, a supermarket nearby, you are more blessed than 99% of the world's population.

Give thanks to GOD.

Enjoy the day.

Happy Thanksgiving from The Meltons, Clarene and BJ

Thought for the day Nov. 24, 2017

I remember when I bought my first computer.

It was a small portable for $398.

I stood in line with several hundred other suckers at Radio Shack, waiting for 12 o'clock midnight, Black Friday's magic hour.

I was younger then, much younger, 35 years younger.

Today, Black Friday is just an Icon, a memory. My shopping, now, is done, sitting right here. No parking problem, no walking all over, no standing in line. I don't even need money. Credit card works just fine. Anything I want is right here and will be delivered to my front door, clothes, shoes, furniture, ink for my printer, even groceries, if I want.

Black Friday, along with walk-in department stores, is at the funeral home, being prepped for burial. Kinda sad to see it go, but Que Sera Que Sera!

Thought for the day Nov. 26, 2017

Procrastination

IT is So hard to say, so easy to do.

Sometimes life can be cruel.

Many think procrastination is sinful. Some people think of it as a cruel word or as a thief "Procrastination is the thief of time".

I think Procrastination gets a bum rap.

For me it is a best friend.

Sometimes when I have a discussion with my wife, Clarene, I put off my chance to have the last word until tomorrow, maybe 'til next week.

Procrastination brings peace and tranquility.

I look at my yard. It is covered with leaves.

I think I should rake and bag them. Then, I think again. I need a nap.

The leaves will be there tomorrow, Maybe the wind will blow them away.

Then, there is my garage.

Is really does need an overhaul.

In fact, it has needed an overhaul for years. Come to think of it, the garage may be the reason I have perfected Procrastination.

It is always "Maybe tomorrow". I have learned to procrastinate so well, I may be late for my own funeral. Now, don't get me wrong.

Sometimes Procrastination is a bad thing, like when you are on the last roll of toilet tissue. But mostly, I can't say enough nice things about my best friend.

Thought for the Day Nov. 27, 2017

Actions have consequences

ORNERY 'HONORABLE' CONGRESS PEOPLE! HOW MANY MORE LIKE THESE? HOW MANY TAX DOLLARS SPENT TO SAVE THEIR HIDES?

'Ashamed' Franken says he won't quit Senate

JOKE!

© U.S. Senator Al Franken,"**Giant of the Senate**".

"I'm embarrassed and ashamed.

I've let a lot of people down and I'm hoping

I can make it up to them and gradually regain their trust,"

Question: Is he embarrassed and ashamed because he got Religion,

Or because he got caught?

66 year old pervert.

Rep. John Conyers, D-Mich., stepped down as
Ranking Member of the House Judiciary Committee on Sunday
amid an ongoing House Ethics Committee
investigation of sexual harassment allegations.
(Nancy Pelosi's ICON)

88 year old pervert.

Thought for the day Nov. 28, 2017

Imagination with so-called "sexual harassment" charges flooding the market these days, I thought the following 'old' thought for the day might make appropriate reading.

Imagination can be funny, cruel, slanderous, or just meant to deceive.

Flash Back to Oct. 14, 2016

With all the supposed confessions coming out about Donald Trump, I was reminded of an event in my life that I have never told anyone about before.

Sic 'Em Donald!

Now that I am old, grey and harmless, I think you might be amused with my story. This was in 1965 when I was a 40-year-old man, still in the prime of life. Actually, it was on a Monday, July 19. I remember it well. It was etched in my mind. I was flying from Dallas to Chicago on a Braniff 707.

We always rode first class, wore suits and ties, and on this flight, (I know you won't believe it,) I found myself sitting beside Marilyn Monroe!!! Well, I was flabbergasted and speechless. What does a hick from the backwoods of East Texas say to a beautiful famous woman like Marilyn? Fortunately, or maybe unfortunately, Marilyn was a talker. So, a conversation began. You know, like who am I, where am I going? Am I married? Then, am I happily married, etc. Then she told me what good friends she and Robert F. Kennedy were. From there it seemed like she really liked me, and I began to get nervous. About half way through the flight, she reached over and put her hand on my leg. Words cannot describe what went through my mind, or the exhilaration I felt. I began sweating like a stuck pig and my mind was racing a mile a minute. Like I said I was just a 40-year-old man, married, with children, and I didn't need this kind of temptation!!! I didn't want to make a scene. I didn't want to hurt her feelings by telling her to get her hand off my leg. (besides I guess I was flattered). We landed in Chicago. When we got up from our seats, she kissed me on the mouth. I must have turned 10 shades of red and the other passengers started whooping, laughing and clapping their hands. We walked arm in arm as we got off the plane. I start sweating again, profusely, and I am thinking "How am I going to get out of this?'" The Lord said I would not be tempted beyond what I can stand and

I am thinking "Lord, where are you?'" As we walked into the terminal, lo and behold, there was her sometimes boyfriend, Bobby Kennedy, and she left me standing there.

I never saw her again.

The Lord did not forsake me. Now you can see why I never told anybody. Nobody would believe me anyway, and neither should you. This was all a fantasy, just like that 74-year-old grandmother that accused Donald of molesting her on an airplane while she was sitting in a first-class seat 30 years ago. Marilyn died in 1962.

SIC 'EM DONALD!

14 - Harassment

Thought for the day Dec. 2, 2017

Harassment

I read somewhere, today, that a Senator, (I am not sure whether male of female) will soon be introducing a bill titled "All Paws Off". (APO.)

But Elizabeth Warren plans to _filibuster_ the bill, and simultaneously co-sponsor a bill with Al Franken named "No Barred Caresses". (NBC) Bless her heart. I guess she still, after all these years, holds out hope for a little excitement.

SIC 'EM DONALD!!

THOUGHT FOR THE DAY, DEC.11, 2017

Harassment

There is so much fake news these days, it really makes it difficult to have an original thought that is not tainted by fake news. There is even a contest going on to see which news agency can come up with the fakest fake news.

I surmise this is to pull a cloud over millions of sexual harassment charges being brought against famous people, mainly by women. The best one I have heard showed up today. It seems Donald trump, years ago, was riding on an elevator with several people, one of which was a woman that had done something good. She said Donald kissed her on the lips and congratulated her. What she did not say happened, but what did happen is, she was thrilled and appreciative of his congratulation. Years later, after thoughtfully remembering the incident, she stated today that she was HARASSED.

I guess, now that she realizes it, (without realizing it), she has been going through this emotional trauma for all these years, and will now need psychiatric care, she can sue Donald for millions!!!!!

Hogwash!

SIC 'EM DONALD!!!

Thought for the day Dec. 12, 2017

WORD OF THE YEAR

harass [huh-ras, har-uh s]

Harassable, harasser, harassingly, harassment, over harass... This word today is on the lips of nearly everybody. What does it mean when a harasser approaches a harass-able subject and harassingly ogles the subject, then gets sued for harassment?

Are we killing Romance?

I remember growing up, and experiencing, the joy of flirting, THE EXCITEMENT! The ecstasy of my first kiss, holding hands, a runaway heartbeat, sweating hands, hugging and being hugged.

I know I am a fortunate individual because I <u>still</u> experience all these things with my sweet wife, Clarene. God built into ALL living things the undeniable urge and need to propagate. In man's case, it all starts with temptation, then romance, followed by propagation. It will continue, for eons, DESPITE THE DANGER OF BEING SUED FOR "HARASSMENT". Maybe next year LOVE will be word of the year.

THOUGHT FOR THE DAY DEC. 14, 2017
Nothing new under the sun

So, what is new today, I asked myself. I read the paper, checked the internet, listened to TV news.

There was much about tax cuts. Not new.

There was Mueller's collusion investigation. Not new.

There was Roy Moore's lynching. Not new.

Fake story about Paul Ryan resigning. Not new.

Distortion of a Trump tweet. Not new.

Democrats screaming about calamity of Tax Cuts. Not new.

California seceding from the Union. Not new.

Amazon teasing States about new Mammoth Depot and 50,000 new employees.

NFL and kneeling mess. Not new.

Nancy Pelosi showing off her senility. Not new.

Several Congressional committees vowing to fix something. Not new. Never do.

Will John McCain be the Grinch that kills the Christmas tax bill? Not new. Sorry. No news to day. Just more of the same old ....

SIC 'EM DONALD!

15 - Circus

Thought for the day Dec. 16, 2017
Washington, DC Circus

Welcome to the laughable Washington, DC Circus.

We got elephants, donkeys, clowns, and high wire escape artists.

Remember old Jim Clapper, today's P.T. Barnum and Pinocchio.

Pinocchio started this mess about Russia, Russia, Russia. He said 17, count 'em, 17 intelligence agencies agreed the Russians threw the election to Trump. Later, he admitted lying.

Next comes Head Clown playboy, Peter Strzok, husband of a "Melissa Hodgman", and writer of thousands of Love notes to his mistress, Lisa Page. Peter thought he was also the James Bond of the FBI, dedicated to saving America from itself.

Peter did not like Donald Trump. Peter hated Donald Trump.

Trump is stupid! Trump is an idiot!

Peter said he had to prevent Trump from being President.

He and Lisa had a plan. He caused millions of dollars of FBI and DNC money, to be spent trying to derail the Trump Presidential campaign. Peter helped Jim Comey give Hillary a 'stay out of jail card'.

Peter, (James Bond), as a Key <u>Intelligent</u> Intelligence Official, set out to make sure Hillary won.

In the Old Testament of the Bible there is a story about Samson.

Samson was extremely strong, as long as he had long hair.

His enemies hired Delilah to find out his secret.

They had a love affair and Samson finally told her.

Then when he was asleep, she cut his hair and his great strength left him.

His enemies captured him and put out his eyes.

Peter Strzok had great strength as an <u>Intelligent</u> Intelligence Official.

Lisa, in a sense, cut Peter's hair.

He is now captured and buried somewhere deep in the department, just an insignificant government employee.

Trump is President. So, now, who is stupid? Who is the idiot?

There many other clowns, and a herd of 'donkeys', in the circus. Trump is the ringmaster, popping the whip.

SIC 'EM DONALD!

Thought for the day Dec. 17, 2017

TO: XXXXXX XXXX, Writer for the Dallas Morning News

December 17, 2017

GUTTER TALK

Several months ago, you had an editorial about abortion of babies and "Planned Parenthood". You indicated it was a woman's choice to have her baby cut from the womb, its head crushed, dismembered, and thrown in the garbage. It is just the price the baby has to pay for the mother's supreme Ecstasy and pleasure 9 months prior.

I asked you at the time if you could be the one who does the butcher job. You never responded, but after reading your trip to the gutter in today's paper, I believe you would have no problem handling the slaughter and might even relish the opportunity.

I have been reading about all the celebrities and famous people being accused of harassing women. Hundreds have been accused, most of them are your Socialist Democrats friends, and some Republicans.

But accusation and reality are not always the same.

Harassing, as defined today, is bad and should not be tolerated.

However, since Adam and Eve, FLIRTING has been a favorite past time for Men AND Women. That is how a romance gets started.

That is how I convinced my wife to marry me.

Check the definition of Flirting and you will see what is considered HARASSING today.

BUT I HAVE SAID THIS BECAUSE TODAY YOU SET YOURSELF

UP ON THE HIGH GROUND, JUDGING AND CONDEMNING SOME PEOPLE YOU DO NOT KNOW PERSONALLY, WHILE IGNORING A HORDE OF OTHERS WHO HAVE BEEN CAUGHT WITH THEIR HANDS IN THE COOKIE JAR.

You referred to President Trump as the cannibal-in-chief. What on earth does that mean? He eats people? Sick statement.

Are you a saint sent to earth to be judge and jury and sentence pronouncer?

It is true the GOP needs to seek higher moral ground. All of America does. But I would suggest that before you judge others, you lift yourself and other Socialist Democrats out of the gutter. Put your own house in order. Finally, what I have said is not nice and I don't mean to judge you, but if your dissertation today is a mirror image of who you really are, then you are not a nice person.

BJ Melton

Thought for the Day Dec. 21, 2017
Taxes!

For over two years, I have been hearing about Congress rewriting our tax code and reducing my tax bill. Yesterday, December 20, the Republicans in Congress finally passed the Tax Reduction Bill,

WITHOUT A SINGLE "FOR" VOTE BY THE DEMOCRATS. Makes me wonder why Democrats would vote against me keeping more of my own money.

And I have to ask, "What kind of people ARE these that think they can spend my money better than I can?" This is just one of several reasons I COULD NEVER BE A DEMOCRAT! Amen.

SIC 'EM DONALD!

Thought for the day Dec. 22, 2017
Funny

Seriousness aside................

Yesterday, December 21, was the shortest day of the year,

and, quite obviously, the longest night followed. You have never seen your face, and never will, only pictures and mirror reflections, The back of your head either.

My Great Granddaughter, Elli, is now 3 1/2 years old.

She has been going to bible study class for several weeks. Kids this age are like a sponge and soak up knowledge. The only problem is we don't realize what they are soaking up. They watch adults, other kids, and hear words. They tend to mimic actions they see and repeat words they hear, good or bad.

Sometimes this results in something funny--or NOT so funny.

You know that, I know. This is a funny Elli story.

Recently Elli had her first sleep-over with her Grandmother. At 6:30 AM she was awake, jumping on the bed, Yelling "Wake up. We gonna have pancakes and bacon in bed!" My daughter woke up and said "OH, Lord, help me! "To which Elli replied

" The Lord can't help you. He is too busy helping other people!" "Get up!"

Our vines have tender grapes. Be careful. Handle with care.

16 – Christmas 2017

Thought for Christmas day, 2017
Christmas

Christmas, I think, was invented to give special thanks for Jesus birth, but in the whole scheme of things, his sacrifice and resurrection are for what we should be most grateful. As I reflect on the past year, and my whole life for that matter, I realize I have been blessed beyond measure. I count the "Presents" under my tree, My Health, the Love I share with my sweet wife, Clarene, with my family, with my Step family, and my many friends. I have so much, and I am so richly blessed. Every day I thank God for Jesus and ask Him to walk with us, hold our hand, and protect us.

But, sadly, there under my tree, is this lump of coal. I ask God to take it away, but there is no answer. Then Reality and Humility tell me, life is not perfect. Like a rose bush, the flower is beautiful and the aroma wonderful, but the thorns hurt.

Thankfully, under that tree, is a present from Christ, i.e., a promise of Eternal Life, carefully wrapped and freely given.

Merry Christmas everybody.

Thought for the day Dec. 26, 2017
Funny

Yesterday was Christmas. and here we are.

This is today....

The tomorrow.........

You asked for yesterday..........

Is life more good? Will you do What you should? Will you return presents for cash or credit to decrease your debit? Or are you sorry for what you ate, that added to your weight? Maybe you can diet!!

FAT CHANCE!

(File under "All things stupid")

Thought for the Day January 2, 2018
Funny

What am I thinking? Well, not much.

Thinking for the last 3 years has about done me in. And you say "You only had, at best, one thought a day, sometimes none. So, what wore you out?"

Well, someday when you are old and grey, walking with a cane, you will find thinking is a lost art. Knowing, for sure, what day of the week it is, becomes problematic. And if you don't take a daily newspaper, you won't know what the day of the month is.

But, happily, you won't really care, or even think about it.

As for me, I don't think I am senile yet, (maybe a little),

However, I am told we will not know when senility comes calling. So, my advice is to practice being happy, while you still know what HAPPY is.

Happy is where I am at age 92.

Will you be happy today and tomorrow?

Next year?

Anytime?

**I hope you have a
HAPPY New Year!**

Thought for the Day January 3, 2018
New words?

I got up this morning, checked the stock market-DOWN.

Checked my blood pressure-UP.

Turned-on English-speaking TV channel.

But what do I hear? Strange stuff. They are talking about 'Deep State', our beautiful Capitol run over with alligators, collusion, then colluded collusion, harassment, and DACA?

Things that are strange to me. I hear about many colluders, liars, thieves, leakers, 'fake news' media, that should be in jail, but they are out walking the street, like honest people like you and me.

Then I hear about 'sanctuary' cities and a 'sanctuary' STATE. What does that mean? I looked it up.

A sanctuary is a sacred place, such as a shrine. So, as of January 1, 2018, California has been declared a Sacred State. Felons, criminals of all kind, illegal immigrants, (like the many colluders, liars, thieves, leakers, 'fake news' media people in DC), are out walking the street, like you and me.

Sound like a wonderful, peaceful place, a real <u>Shangri la</u>! Whoopee!

Now here is a place my thoughts that can get me in trouble.

Suddenly, running through my mind are questions.

Like "What makes a felon a felon"? "What makes a thief a thief?" "What makes a killer, a killer?" "What does illegal mean?" To be a felon, thief, or killer, somebody gets hurt.

Who is that somebody? Why, it is you and me, the innocent, the honest.

Tough, Buddy. We don't count.

Finally, I have to ask, "If <u>Shangri la</u> is good for California and DC, why not all 50 states?'

No. Thanks but no thanks!!

2nd Thought Jan. 3, 2018
Self-explanatory

Thought for the day Jan. 4, 2018
Crazy?

I look at the people in DC, New York, California, Chicago, Dallas, Europe, Far East, Mid-East, Asia, and N. Korea, and I wonder "Is everybody crazy?" Then I think, 'How do you measure 'crazy'?

Who determines what 'sane' is?

I remember saying to someone in my past "You're crazy!" Come to think about it, I said that yesterday about Jerry Brown and his California "Sanctuary State". Obviously, since I am sane myself, I can make that judgement. But then, being a sane and 'reasonable' "thinking" person, I ask "What is the criteria for determining 'sanity'?

"Who developed the criteria"?

The definition of "SANE" is 'someone who is sane, of sound mind'. What on earth does that say? This gets messy. What would qualify anyone to be a judge of sanity? Maybe I don't want to go there. It is beginning to warp my 'sane' mind.

Finally, it could be that everybody is crazy except me and thee, and sometimes I wonder about thee! AMEN

Thought for the day January 5, 2018
Crazy?

In the Sanctuary State of California, is it still illegal to rob a bank, or is it just an undocumented withdrawal?

To me, since California has been proclaimed a Sanctuary State, the Kate Steinle story needs to be told, over and over again.

How many other 'Kate Steinle stories' will be washed into San Francisco Bay?

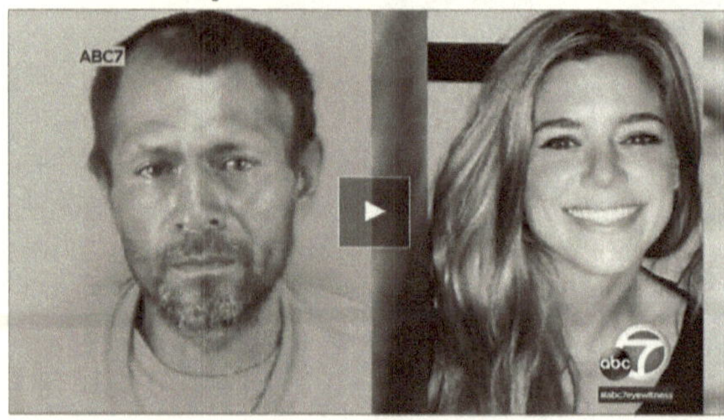

Juan Francisco López-Sánchez Zarate: or Kate Steinle age 32 years

Juan Jose Dominguez de la Parra; or

Garcia Zarate

Dead, killed by gunshot

 RAP SHEET

Born in Mexico, 45 years old, but maybe 52.

Illegal immigrant, 5 times deported

Current location California Sanctuary State (perhaps)

7 felony convictions, Drug dealer, Thief

March 26, 2015 in jail, felony convictions for drug dealing.

April 15, 2015 (20 days later) RELEASED from jail, slate cleaned!!!

 July 1, 2015 (77 days later) Killed Kate Steinle with stolen gun

(Gun stolen from HOMELAND SECURITY GUARD'S CAR)

Dec1., 2017, (28 MONTHS LATER) Convicted of 'illegal possession of firearm'.

Sentence: Promise not to do this again.

Deported a sixth time? Maybe, maybe not?

Still in Sanctuary State? Maybe.

Eligible to vote? Probably.

On January 1, 2018, Jerry Brown, Governor of California, acting as GOD, sanctified thousands of people like JUAN.

Is he CRAZY?

BUILD THE WALL!!

17 – Fake News

Thought for today January 8, 2018

Fake news, Propaganda

I have asked you many times to beware of fake news and propaganda.

I sent you this thought on Aug. 4, 2016, well before the election.

"Thought for the day Aug. 4, 2016"

Put your seat belts on. Charges against Donald Trump, innuendos, inferences, allegations, accusations, lies, TV ads, and propaganda you can't imagine at this point, have now begun to increase in intensity.

Where they will go no one knows, but the billionaires with their hands in the cookie jar will not give up easily.

Below is one example of STUFF that showed up Wednesday. Rep. Karen Bass, an ultra-liberal California Democrat in her 3rd term, on Wednesday launched a change.org petition calling for Donald Trump to a undergo mental health evaluation, insinuating he may have NPD,

Narcissistic Personality Disorder, (like Obama has.)

Her qualifications to make this charge: She is a member of the black caucus in Congress and she was once a physician's assistant.

PS: She also introduced a bill in Congress to rename a post office. I don't know if it passed."

Today, with his "non-presidential' behavior, the failure to prove collusion with Russia, the Record Stock Market, record unemployment rate, and unbelievable success on many things of importance to Americans, is causing the Democrats, Liberals, Socialists, to go absolutely berserk, wild, crazy, deranged.

Like I said on Aug. 4, 2016, Hang on to your seat belts. BECAUSE OF THEIR FAILURE TO DESTROY TRUMP, DUMP TRUMP, IMPEACH TRUMP, DEFEAT TRUMP, they have become LIKE BANSHEES, screaming, cursing and beating the air! The Democrat party, the RINOs, and the swamp critters are gasping for breath.

In trying to destroy Trump, they are killing themselves.

And what do I say?

They hate My America, so I hope their destruction is fast, painful, and complete.

SIC 'EM DONALD! MAGA!

Thought for the day January 15, 2018

While I have been sitting here, with my mind in neutral, feeling sorry for myself and seeking sympathy, because my son Rick finally went to his reward, the world did not stop.

The Democrats and bleeding-heart liberals, plus many no names intent on destroying our America, are creating a legal and illegal immigration CRISIS!

Think about this. By the end of 2018 there will be 8,000,000,000 (that's billions) people on this earth, most of them poor, illiterate, under nourished, and sickly. America has less than 5% of this number, and we have a great Country. Because of our work ethic, our natural resources, and, I believe, our belief in GOD, we, by world standards, are considered prosperous.

BUT, BUT, BUT, <u>WE!! have millions of poor, illiterate, under nourished, and sickly, living on food stamps, thousands that are homeless living on the street, under bridges, and just wandering around wondering where their next bite of food will come from.</u> And the Democrats "SAY" they want to bring in millions more poor,

illiterate, under nourished, and sickly, that don't speak our language, so the Democrats can get that warm feeling of helping some soul from a foreign country join our millions of poor, illiterate, under nourished, and sickly. Let's face the truth. It is not our fault there are billions of people who are poor, illiterate, under nourished, and sickly. WE CANNOT ADOPT THEM ALL!!! We could try to take care of our own, spending money helping our own poor and homeless.

But what do the Democrats do? In their crazed efforts to demonize and destroy President Trump, they ignore the plank in their own eye, and throw up a smoke screen of 'pretend compassion' for the 'world' poor people, ignoring our own, and, in the process, create hate, division, strife.

Their goal: Destroy Trump and continue the destruction of America that Obama started.

Hate is a bad thing. Do I have a hate feeling? Unfortunately, YES, and it feels good.

SIC 'EM DONALD!!!

Thought for the day January 16, 2018
Identical Twins?

This is a picture of Dick Durbin, Senator from Illinois, and Clown Schumer, Senator from New York.

Legally, they are citizens. They each have two significant attributes, they are greedy and love power.

Elected to represent the citizens of their state, they represent only themselves, and their actions are designed to maintain and enlarge their power base, the cost to you and America being irrelevant.

Turning their back on the millions of poor and homeless Americans,

They choose to fight to bring in POOR AND HOMELESS immigrants, both legal and illegal, and keep our southern border open for anyone to cross.

Selective immigrants, who might contribute to the betterment of America, are not a consideration.

They want you to think they are doing this for humanitarian reasons, helping some unfortunate souls achieve a better life in America.

It is propaganda of the worst kind.

SIMPLY PUT, THEY WANT TO USE YOUR MONEY TO BUY VOTES BY IMMIGRANTS, IN ORDER TO MAINTAIN THEIR POWER BASE, AND THAT OF THE DEMOCRAT-SOCIALIST PARTY.

They camouflage it as kindness and compassion, playing on your heart strings, knowing you were raised to care for the unfortunate.

Really American citizens? More like the devil painting 'nice' pictures. Stay alert. Don't play the 'sucker' game.

SIC 'EM DONALD!!!

Thought for the day Jan. 19, 2018
1.18.2018 GOVERNMENT SHUTDOWN

"We will not leave here without a DACA fix," Pelosi said.

President Trump said " No funding for the wall, no DACA fix.

Hope you brought your sleepers and toothbrush"

Diane Feinstein said "Shutting down the government is a very serious thing.

People die, accidents happen. You don't know. Necessary functions can cease."

(This is the senator who 'mistakenly' released a "classified" document because she

HAD A BAD COLD!)

Diane, I wonder, have you not noticed, people die <u>nearly</u> every day? EVEN WHEN THE GOVERNMENT IS 'OPEN'.???

Why are we not awed by such brilliance!!! AND GET THIS, THEY ARE BOTH FROM THE "SACRED" STATE OF CALIFORNIA.

Sic 'em Donald!!!

Thought for the day Jan. 20, 2018
Schumer shutdown!

This is so disgusting! The military, who eke out a living from paycheck to paycheck, <u>will not get paid.</u>

Our Congressmen, living a life of luxury, will continue to be overpaid and underworked, obviously <u>care more about illegals than our own citizens!</u>

Schumer Shutdown: Senate Democrats <u>Brag</u> About Having Votes to Shut Down Government via Filibuster

Come November we have to make them pay!

SIC 'EM DONALD!!!

My thought for the day Jan. 23, 2018
Sad, but grateful

This morning I sit here with, not one thought, but many thoughts running through my mind.

Much of my night was spent trying to answer QUESTIONS-questions like WHY? and WHY ME? You see, I buried my second child yesterday, my SOLDIER son Rick.

This is not the natural order-
THE YOUNG ARE SUPPOSED TO BURY THE OLD!

So, as I sit here asking questions that have no answers, Life is what it is-memories, what has been, not what will be. Yesterday is now a memory, and one that I will cherish until there are no more tomorrows.

Rick was buried with class. After a short military ceremony, playing of TAPS, the folding of the flag by two handsome young soldiers, and the presentation of the flag to Rick's wife Jeanne, filled me with pride, and thankfulness.

Yes, thankfulness. Thankful, knowing my son, like millions before him, actually gave his life to guarantee a life of freedom for you and me. Then I think about Jesus and the sacrifice HE made for you and me, offering us a chance for life after this life.

I be grateful for one more day.

BJ Melton

18 – Birds of a Feather

Thought for the Day Jan. 24, 2018
Birds of a feather

This may be old news, but it is not fake news. Has to warm your heart and remind you of how thankful we are for Donald trump.

SIC 'EM DONALD

Thought for the day Jan. 26, 2018
WAR ON POVERTY

You are probably asking right now "What brought this up?" Well, it came to mind because of DACA, immigration, illegal immigration, and the Democrat party's determination to keep as many people on the "plantation" as possible, WHICH MEANS POVERTY FOR MILLIONS!

Here is a little history, with comment.

"We have declared unconditional war on poverty. Our objective is total victory. I believe that 30 years from now Americans will look back upon these 1960s as the time of the great American Breakthrough toward the victory of prosperity over poverty," said then-President Lyndon Johnson in 1964. In his January 1964 State of the Union address, President Lyndon Johnson proclaimed, "This administration today, here and now, declares unconditional war on poverty in America."

In the 54 years since that time, U.S. taxpayers have spent over $23 trillion on anti-poverty programs. Adjusted for inflation, this spending (which does not include Social Security or Medicare) is three times the cost of all U.S. military wars since the American Revolution.

Yet progress against poverty, as measured by the U.S. Census Bureau, has been minimal, and in terms of President Johnson's main goal of reducing the "causes" rather than the mere "consequences" of poverty, the War on Poverty has failed completely.

In fact, a significant portion of the population is now less capable of self-sufficiency than it was when the War on Poverty began.

1964 In the 18 to 64-year old age group there were 11,007,000 in poverty (13.7%)

2012 In the 18 to 64-year old age group there were 26,497,000 in poverty (10.5%)

2016 Total number in poverty 40.6 million

Does welfare, when all is said and done, really help solve the problem of poverty?

Apparently not.

BUT...........several hundred thousand Federal employees of the 92+ Welfare agencies are doing very well, most them Civil Service employees drawing a handsome salary, and looking for ways to spend more 'welfare' money. One agency advertises for new clients, telling people we can help you get some free money. Just call this number #______________.

So, approximately 40% of money available disappears into the bowels of bureaucrats.

BUILD THE WALL, DONALD!!!

Thought for the day Jan. 28, 2018

Scam!! Please note

(This is unrelated to the sale on line of my Book)

Yesterday I checked my bank account and found a surprise. On Friday Jan. 26 there was a "debit" charge for $34.99 to eBook store, and it was to be a monthly charge!!!!

Never heard of it and the only time 'debit' shows on my bank account is for company insurance.

I sent a message to my Bank and got answer explaining where it came from with a telephone # to call.

I called, got voice mail. Left belligerent message.

Called bank #. Explained problem and they initiated a dispute. Later someone for eBook store called. I repeated belligerent message, only louder. Told him it was scam, he knows it is a scam, and my bank was filing a dispute. He then said he would cancel the charge.

All well and good, BUT........... How were they able to charge directly to my bank account? without any authorization? And I wonder, why did my bank accept it without my authorization?

Did they generate a false authorization somehow?

Be alert for scams. They are Multiple!!

Scary

BJ Melton

Thought for tonight, Jan. 30, 2018
Words

Tonight, I listened to President Trump give his State of the Union speech. And I am amazed at the many things that have been done to improve our country. The list is long, and I hope you heard it. There was much clapping of hands by Republicans and other Americans.

But it was depressing, but not unexpected, that Democrats sat on their butts, saying to America and the world "WE don't want to make America better"!

Looked like a bunch of dummies. Easy to see why they chose

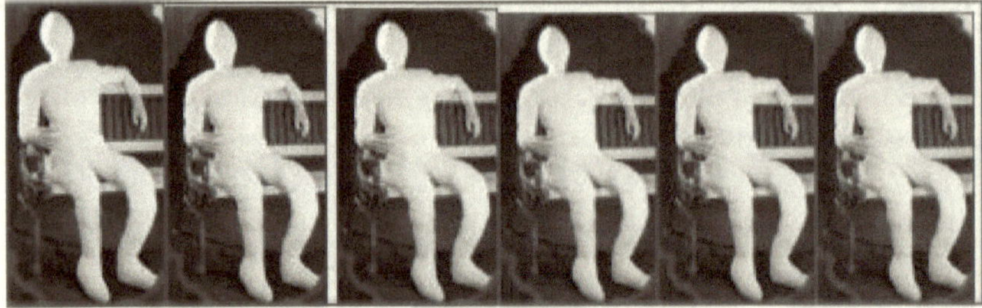

The donkey as their party symbol. Afterward I listened to part of the Democrat rebuttal by another Kennedy. It quickly became apparent that he, like President Kennedy, has mastered the art of double talk.

He mouthed nice words and phrases, feel good stuff, which, when analyzed, had no substance. He will be a hero in the state of Massachusetts. I thought going to bed would be a better use of my time.

SIC 'EM DONALD!!!

19 – State of the Union

Thought for today, Jan. 31, 2018

STATE OF THE UNION

Today, the news from the media, is, as you would expect,

STUPID!

It barely mentions the pluses, and when it does, it is critical-should have been better. But it spares no words when it emphasizes his exaggerations as lies.

Such as "employees have received $1000's and $1000's in bonuses". In reality, it has been Millions and Millions. Supposedly, he lied about exporting oil, when we still import some oil.

But what he said was "We are an ENERGY exporter". We are 'exporting' millions of barrels of Liquid Natural Gas (LGN) to Europe, Asia, and South America, so we are a net "energy exporter"!

All this does is confirm that the 'media' lives and dies on lies, lies, and 'fake' news.

The "Dump Trump" movement is still alive, but sick and badly crippled.

10 or 12 Democrats skipped the Address to <u>punish</u> Trump

This was one of them: Did you miss her?

Did you miss any of them?

SIC 'EM DONALD!!!

Thought for the day Feb. 1, 2018

Historic photograph just recovered.

Democrats on morning of November 8, 2016. Look closely and you will see Queen Hillary, Clown Schumer, Maxine Waters, and Nancy Pelosi.

He who laughs last, laughs best!
SIC 'EM DONALD!!!

Thought for the day Feb. 2, 2018
Russia, Russia, Russia
The Memo! The Memo! The Memo!
   Today is the day an earthquake hits Washington, DC The swamp critters will be running for their holes.
   But there is no place to hide.
SIC 'EM DONALD!!!

20 – The Memo

Thought for the day Feb. 3, 2018

THE MEMO!

In summary The Memo:
1. Proves there was collusion.
2. The DNC and Clinton campaign colluded with key DOJ and FBI officials to:
3. Produce a dossier designed to discredit Trump
4. The DNC, Clinton campaign, AND FBI paid good money for false information.
5. False info was used to obtain warrant to spy on Trump campaign
6. False info was used to appoint special counsel, Mueller.
7. Mueller charged to investigate "collusion" of Trump people with Russia.
8. Mueller is illegally spending tax money chasing a rabbit down a hole.
9. Crimes were committed. A number of people have earned long prison sentences.
10. Trump and his people are squeaky clean.

SIC 'EM DONALD!!!

Thought for the day Feb. 4, 2018

The Memo cont'd

I read enough of the Socialist Dallas news this morning to know that Fake news is alive but sick.

The Obama-Clinton Democrats in the FBI and DOJ have been exposed for what they _are_, for what they _did_, and for _who they are._ And they are saying Conservatives in Congress are guilty of exposing them and causing American to lose faith in our Justice department.

"If Hillary had won, (sob), you conservatives would never have known what you 'claim' we did.

"It's not our fault!!" "It's your fault we got caught!"

"Shame on you!"

Reminds me of the jersey cow we had when I was a boy. When she did her thing, she deposited a big cow 'pie', and it stunk. After a while it would crust over and not stink.

In July of 2016 Comey and his cohorts in crime deposited a huge cow 'pie'. It crusted over.

Finally, in late 2017, the Republicans started stirring the 'pie' and the stink was back, worse than ever. And today we have the MEMO, and the stink IS ALL THE REPUBLICANS FAULT!

YOU STIRRED THE 'PIE'!

FAKE NEWS!

SIC 'EM DONALD!!!

Thought for the day Feb. 5, 2018
Important things

Yesterday the New England Patriots and the Philadelphia Eagles played in the "Superbowl".

I think the score was 41-33 Eagles won. Last year the _______________ and the _______________ played in the "Superbowl" and the ____________ won with a score of ____________. Now why can't I remember what happened a year ago? The "Superbowl" is so important!!! Maybe it is not on my list of important things.

After the last round of golf, I played, I could tell you every shot I made, with what club and what happened to the ball.

Today, I can't remember the last time I played. At the time it was so important, but I guess it was really not one of the important things in my life.

So, what is important enough to remember?

What are my values?

What are your values? Think about it.

Thought for the day Feb. 7, 2018
Desperate SUCKER!

The guy shown below, Adam Schiff, is an ultra-liberal Democrat (what else) from the sacred state of California, who aspires of running for President in 2020. Currently he is fanatical about discrediting or embarrassing President Trump. President Trump now has on his desk the Democrat version of the MEMO!

It is designed as a trap for Donald.

Will he redact the lies, giving the Democrats more ammunition to scream "Foul"?

Will he stop the release?

Or, will he declassify it, as is, sharing their lies with all Americans?

NOW FOR THE CRUX OF THIS THOUGHT. Recently, there was fake news about Trump and a Russian model. Where did it come from?

Sic 'Em Donald!

DESPERATE SUCKER

Spoofed: In April 2017, Adam Schiff, the ranking Democratic member of the House "Intelligence" Committee, had a seven-minute conversation with Russian comedians who offered him fake 'kompromat' including naked pictures of the president, which he said he would report to the FBI.

Russian pranksters:

Vladimir 'Vovan' Kuznetsov, 30, and Alexei 'Lexus' Stolyarov, 28, called Schiff and persuaded him to stay on the call for seven minutes as they outlined their fake claims.

SIC 'EM DONALD!

Sad thought for today Feb. 8, 2018

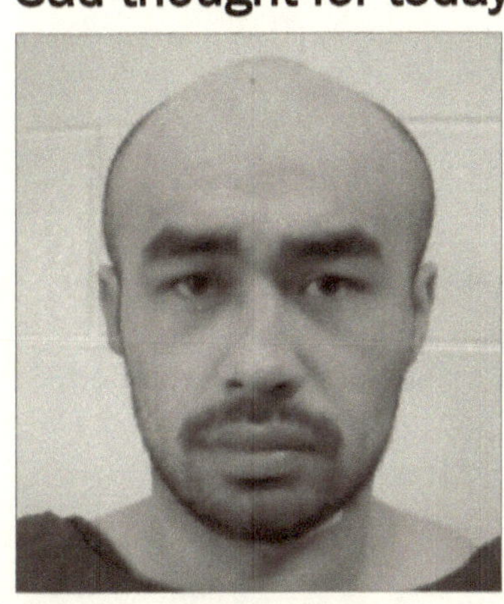

Yesterday this "man" was walking the street.

Today, he is in jail, charged with Capital murder of a 15-year veteran of the Richardson Police Department, and a civilian.

He is 26 years old with a record of nothing but trouble.

2009: arrested for stealing a car

2010: arrested on a drug possession charge 2016: Richardson Police arrested him for possession of controlled substance, given 2 years' probation 2017: Plano Police arrested him for possession of a controlled substance, given 2 years' probation. He will now be held in jail for months, his mental condition evaluated, probably more than once, his unfortunate environmental upraising microscopically scrutinized, bleeding heart Liberals will blame others for him murdering a police officer and for being a druggie.

He may, eventually, be tried. His verdict?

Finally, the innocent gun will be blamed for firing the fatal shots, so, we need more gun control!!!

Lost in all of this will be the sickness that has invaded America since Madeline O'Hair, the atheist, was successful in running GOD out of schools, and OBAMA was partially successful in getting GOD and bibles out of everything. There is probably a lesson to be learned from this event and many others just like it.

What do you think it might be?

Our degenerating moral fiber?

Subtle hints of future trouble?

Has murdering unborn children cheapened the meaning of life? Think about it.

Thought for the day Feb. 14, 2018
ORGANIC STUFF? Scam?

Today is Valentine's day. If you have a Sweetie, and you honor her/him today, you do good. As for me and my Sweetie, every day is Valentine's Day.

But now I am thinking about something else, scams. Yesterday, I went to the store. One item on my list was ground black pepper. I found a small can of organic pepper. Price $6.99. I found a large can of 'just pepper' for $2.99.

Over twice as much for half the price.

Scam.

Then I checked eggs. Regular eggs on special- $.99 doz.

Organic eggs-$4.29 doz.

Scam.

In all of my 92 years, I have never 'knowingly' purchased anything that "qualified' as 'organic'.

Why, I asked myself, is organic worth paying a premium price?

Taste? no. Insurance for a healthy and longer life? No. Then, I learn, many claims of 'organic' stuff, are really not 'organic' at all.

Just a scam.

Tomorrow learn about "~~Global warming~~" Climate change.

Scam.

21 – Climate Change

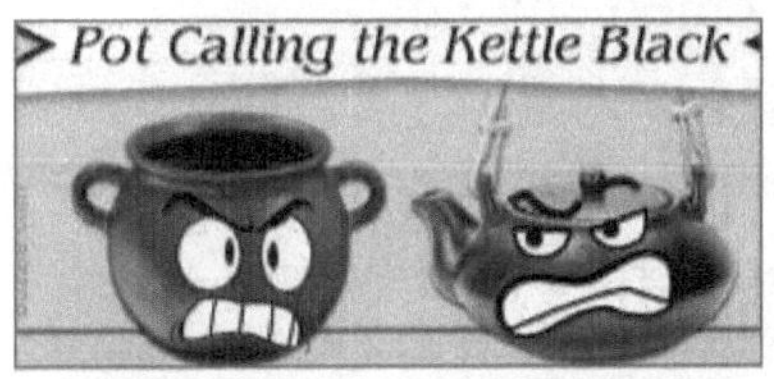

Thought for the day Feb. 15, 2018

Climate change

Climate change can wait!

Yesterday, Nicolas Cruz murdered 17 school children. Yesterday, Nicolas Cruz fulfilled his promise to be a PROFESSIONAL SCHOOL KILLER. In September 1977, the FBI was alerted to a YouTube comment posted by Nicolas Cruz, that his goal was to be a PROFESSIONAL SCHOOL KILLER.

6 months later, on Valentine's Day, he successfully achieved his goal. Now there are questions.

Consider known information.

He was a known trouble maker.

He was ejected from school.

He dressed weird.

He had many guns and bragged about them.

The FBI had a warning of:

His goal to be a Professional School killer.

What is not known.

How did he manage to accumulate his arsenal?

What did the FBI do in the 6 months after being warned?

Does he have parents, or was he cloned from an ape?

Is he a druggie?

Where did he get money for a car and guns?

Why did he set such a goal for himself?

To all this, I have a comment, factitious though it may be. "If the FBI and DOJ officials in Washington, D.C., had been more concerned with doing FBI and DOJ work, rather than trying to destroy President Trump, would this have been prevented?"

If you see something, say something!

SIC 'EM DONALD!!!

Thought for the day Feb. 16, 2018
Civilization - Contemplate this

> Before our white brothers arrived to make us civilized men, we didn't have any kind of prison. Because of this, we had no delinquents. Without a prison, there can be no delinquents. We had no locks nor keys and therefore among us there were no thieves. When someone was so poor that he couldn't afford a horse, a tent or a blanket, he would, in that case, receive it all as a gift. We were too uncivilized to give great importance to private property. We didn't know any kind of money and consequently, the value of a human being was not determined by his wealth. We had no written laws laid down, no lawyers, no politicians, therefore we were not able to cheat and swindle one another. We were really in bad shape before the white men arrived and I don't know how to explain how we were able to manage without these fundamental things that (so they tell us) are so necessary for a civilized society.
>
> –John Fire Lame Deer

We know North Korea is not civilized and we say something must be done to civilize them. They have people starving, people in prison, people being killed in the streets, and people in high places making the rules.

So, we take the high road and appoint ourselves the caretaker of the world.

WE ARE CIVILIZED.

WE MUST CIVILIZE THEM!!

Then we turn a blind eye to our starving homeless people, our prisons full of people, people being killed in the streets of Florida, Chicago, Las Vegas, and people in high places making rules for us to follow. SEE THE DIFFERENCE?

Thought for the day Feb. 18, 2018
My new friend, Lotty!

Yesterday was a different day, not like most days.

At about 8:30 AM I found myself in the midst of about a

1000 Republicans who think like me. The event was an America First meeting featuring Vice President Mike Pence as our speaker. I found a seat on the 4th row (1st two rows reserved) next to a lovely lady named Lotty. We discovered we had much in common, so, I told her about my book 'My America is Back" and she wanted to order one and we exchanged information. We are now Social Media friends. That was good fortune # 1.

Ken Paxton, Texas's Lt. Governor participated in a panel discussion, before Mike Pence talked.

After the panel discussion, Paxton sat down on the row in front of us.

At the conclusion of Pence's talk, he emphasized "America is Back".

Sounded like my book's name!

Then he came down to the fence set up to separate him from the crowd, and Lotty headed straight to him with me right behind.

On the way, I shook hands with Ken Paxton and gave him a flyer about my book.

I told him he needed to order one and get one for Donald Trump.

He said he would. Could be good fortune #2.

Then Lotty got to Pence and was quick to tell him about my book. Then I shook hands with him and gave him a flyer. He said he would order a book and make sure Trump got one.

Could be good fortune #3.

Then on the way to valet for my car, a lady stopped me. She heard us talking about my book, wanted to know more about it. I had carried 3 flyers with me, hoping what happened, would happen. I gave her the third one and she promised to tell all her friends.

Good fortune #4.

While I was waiting on my car, Lotty and her husband were waiting also. So, we talked some more. For some reason, I had a book in my car. I told Lotty, and she bought it on the spot. I autographed it for, 'My new best friend', and we went on our way, me on cloud nine.

SIC 'EM DONALD!!! MAGA!!!

Thought for the day Feb. 19, 2018

Harassment

I read today where the Democrats are planning a campaign for this year's election, emphasizing all the women who claim to have been harassed in my Donald Trump in the last 20-30 years.

It reminded me of this famous quote: "Hell Hath No Fury Like A Woman Scorned"

So, what does it really mean?

Hell: traditionally depicted as a place of perpetual fire where the wicked are punished after death.

BJ Melton

Fury: wild or violent anger

Scorned: Contempt, disdain, feeling toward a person considered despicable, unworthy. You may have experienced or witnessed a case of fury - i.e. man, vs woman, or woman vs woman.

I know I have, several times in my 92 years and it ain't pretty.

But the classic example we have all observed, is the fury of Hillary Clinton, when so many women became Bill's choice in the bedroom.

She set about to destroy them. Another example, or rather many examples, is when the woman's advances toward a man are rejected, and their feelings are crushed!! Revenge! Revenge! I must get revenge!

So, imagination takes over. Facts become fantasy. Memories of what might have been, become reality.

Now, don't get me wrong. I know men and women can be, and are, guilty of harassment. Harvey Weinstein is one example. Hillary is another. But Congress putting on their HALO? Come on. Congress has spent $millions$ from their "secret" fund, settling Harassment claims against members.

SIC 'M DONALD!! MAGA!!!

22 - Deplorables

Thought for the day Feb. 20, 2018

Trump Supporters are Uneducated
by LeBron James

"At the end of the day, I don't think a lot of people ~~was~~ *were* ^-5^ educated."

"When it becomes vote time, people are just not *awkward* educated on either the individual or what's going on in the state of the world right now."

"And am I saying that the people of Ohio ~~wasn't~~ *aren't* ^-5^ educated? Am I saying that some of the other states that voted for him ~~was~~ *are* ^-5^ uneducated?"

"I've done things for my daughter and realized I shouldn't have ~~gave~~ *given* ^-5^ my daughter that many damn Skittles."

LeBron, please see me after class

Deplorables

LeBron James thinks Hillary's Deplorables are uneducated, NOT educated like he is.

Lebron made millions bouncing a ball.

Everybody knows..............

Being rich makes you wise.

At least in your eyes

Hollywood stars also know it

Their words show it

And politicians, they are soooo smart

Making money is an art Notice Pelosi for sure as she spreads her manure. Burma Shave

SIC 'EM DONALD!!! MAGA!!!

Thought for the day Feb. 22, 2018

17 children dead. Is it Joe's fault?

Did you know that <u>Senator</u> Joe Biden (Obama's VP) in 1990 introduced and had passed the Gun-Free School Zones Act and signed into law in November of 1990? The bill "prohibits any person from knowingly possessing a firearm ... at a place the individual knows, or has reasonable cause to believe, is a school zone". 17 states, today, do NOT comply with this law, but educators in 33 may not arm themselves to protect their students. Nor may schools in these 33 states even hire armed security guards. "You didn't know that?

I bet you don't know this either! Research from the Crime Prevention Research Center shows that every public shooting since at least 1950 in the U.S. in which more than three people have been killed has taken place where citizens are not allowed to carry guns, like Stoneman Douglas High School.

Truism #1 "81% of police officers support arming teachers and principals, so that the real first responders can protect the children."

Truism #2 Crazies may be nuts, but they are not stupid. Crazies who want to shoot up a school, will know beforehand that they will be the only one armed!

Truism #3 Guns are not the problem. The ABSENCE of guns in schools is the problem!

Truism #4 The gunman Cruz has offered to plead guilty to the murder of 17 people, in exchange for life in prison. Why? He is afraid to die.

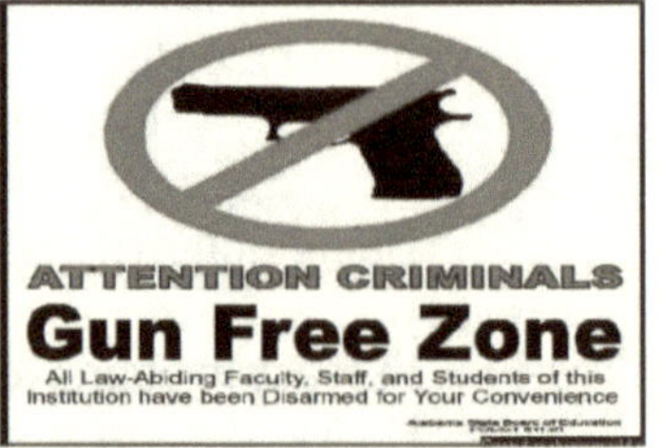

Solution: Repeal 'Uncle Joe's Law" and put 1st responders on the campus!

UNCLE JOE'S SIGN!

For your convenience, no one here is armed.

Thought for the day Feb. 23, 2018

CLIMATE CHANGE?

The National Oceanic and Atmospheric Administration (NOAA) budget for 2018 is $5.7 billion. The budget for the agency's Office of Oceanic and Atmospheric Research, which supports critical climate change research, will increase, by 3.5%, from $462 million to $478 million. This money is awarded by approved 'grants' to universities who, in turn, supplement Professors' income to do research on mostly insignificant things.

One of their favorites these days, is Climate Change. You know, we all know, our climate changes, sometimes by the minute. Been doing it for eons and will continue to do so. Scientists know this, too.

Back in the '90's someone took some data, collected worldwide, and started yelling

"The sky is falling" (We are getting hotter), and the hoax began. Dearly beloved Al Gore wrote a book and made millions. Al knew why we are getting 'warmer', also. It is all that CO_2 we are generating, burning fossil fuels.

So, today, we are spending millions on 'scientific' research trying to prove the warming is manmade. If the data doesn't fit the foregone conclusion, it is discarded as erroneous date. The research (gravy train) must continue. I guess it is only right to keep supplementing the salaries of all these professors. The 'dog' has the bone now and we can't take it away.

I said all that garbage above, to remind you of another 'crisis". Back in the early 1970's we were running out of natural gas, and we had GASOLINE rationing!   How did that turn out?

We, also, were entering a new ice age. The earth was getting colder and without gas to keep us warm, we were headed the way of the dinosaurs, I say with tongue in cheek.

It is kinda funny how we can create a crisis out of nothing. Individually, we do it pretty regularly.

Carbon dioxide is not our enemy. Billions of animals generate tons of it every minute and plants love it. In return, the plants give us oxygen, and we repeat the cycle. God created a perpetual motion machine. Man ain't gonna change it! Think about it.

Thought for the Day March 2, 2018
On being Positive

Yesterday I was upset with Trump. He announced tariffs on steel and aluminum. Knocked my stocks in the head.

Today I am doubly upset with Trump because of the apparent gun deal.

Knocked my stocks in the head.

Now I feel like I have concussion.

But I get to thinking. Many times, Donald has made statements and decisions, and everybody said he was wrong. Later he was proven to be right. Is he really wrong this time? What is his motive? Is this a negotiating ploy of some kind?

I know the swamp critters will jump on any apparent mistake or weakness and propagandize it to the hilt.

So, why don't we just wait a while before condemning him?

He may be right again.

Check this out:

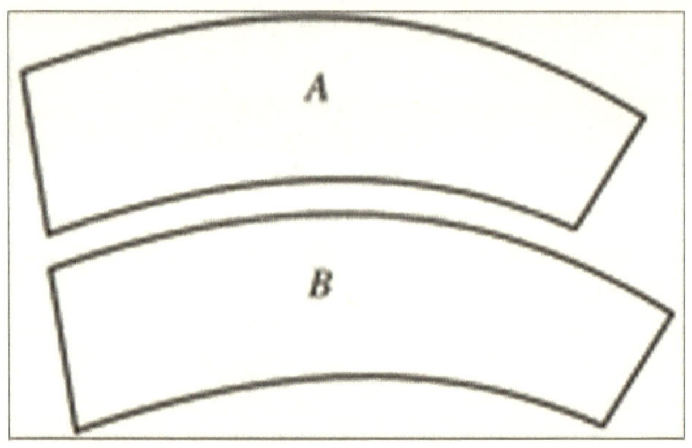

Hard to believe. They are exactly the same size. Next time you are absolutely POSITIVE about something, pause and reconsider.

SIC 'EM DONALD!!!

23 – Simple Stuff

Thought for the day March 6, 2018
Simple stuff

It is elementary. If you don't eat right and exercise, your body goes to pot!

Most people do not eat and exercise properly. Consequently, entrepreneurs have created diets and exercise programs that your lazy self can buy.

This is also elementary. If you feed your brain garbage and do not exercise it, it, too, turns to mush, and senility arrives before it's time.

Today's thought is simple stuff.

What is Brain exercise? Why is it important, and how do we do it? Thinking, it seems to me, is brain exercise. To keep it working, we must think. Right off, you say "No big deal. I think all the time." But do you really?

The brain is like a computer. You can feed it good stuff, bad stuff, or stuff of no consequence. It eats what you feed it. What you 'feed' it, and what you think about, will determine what kind of person you are.

I told you this would be simple.

SO, JUST THINK ABOUT THINKIN ABOUT IT!

Thought for the day March 12, 2018
OUR ELECTORAL COLLEGE ELECTION SYSTEM

I think this is very important information. YOU MAY, ALSO. In their infinite wisdom, the United States' founders created the Electoral College. WHY? <u>To ensure the STATES were fairly represented.</u>

CONSIDER THESE STATISTICS

- *There are 3,141 counties in the United States.*
- *Trump won 3,084 of them.*
- *Clinton won 57.*
- *There are 62 counties in New York State.*
- *Trump won 46 of them.*
- *Clinton won 16.*
- *Clinton won the popular vote by approx. 1.5 million votes.*
- *In the 5 counties that encompass NYC, (Bronx, Brooklyn, Manhattan,*
- *Richmond & Queens)*
- *Clinton received well over 2 million more votes than Trump.*

- *(Clinton won 4 of these counties; Trump won Richmond)*
- *Therefore, these 5 counties alone, more than accounted for Clinton winning the popular vote of the entire country.*
- *These 5 counties comprise 319 square miles.*
- *The United States is comprised of 3,797,000 square miles.*
- *When you have a country that encompasses almost 4 million square miles of territory, it would be ludicrous to even suggest that the vote of those who inhabit a mere 319 square miles should dictate the outcome of a national election.*

Now think about this. Where are most of America's problems located?

Why, NYC, LA, and Chicago of course.

So, ask yourself, would you want the rest of America to be a mirror image of these 3 cities?

Probably not.

Popular vote would have ~~blessed~~ cursed you with Hillary.

SIC 'EM DONALD! MAGA!!!

Thought for the day March 13, 2018

Today, Trump made history. He fired his Secretary of State.

Today, Trump made Three people happy.

Himself

Tillerson

Mike Pompeo

Trump has not been happy with Tillerson.

Tillerson has not been happy with Trump. Tillerson has not smiled in 13 months.

Tillerson smiled today. 

Trump smiled today. 

Pompeo is always smiling. 

SIC 'EM DONALD! MAGA!!!

Thought for the day March 14, 2018

What happened yesterday is just a memory. If you liked it, good.

If it didn't go your way, tough.

Sic 'Em Donald!

Tomorrow, 'today' will be a memory.

Will "today" be a good memory or a bad one? You can start by thanking the Lord for one more day, then having a good or bad day is mostly your choice.

Think about it.

SIC 'EM DONALD! MAGA!!!

24 – I See Stupid People

Thought for the day March 15, 2018

Stupid people

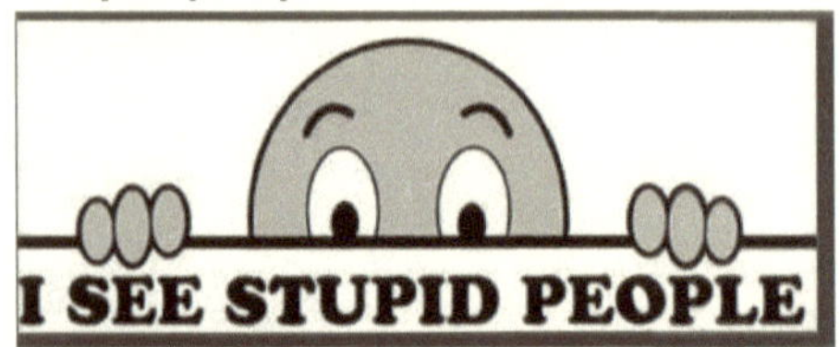

When I look at Congress, this is no more clearly demonstrated than the vote yesterday of 407-10 to pass the "School Safety Bill", by the house of Reps. $500 million over 10 years to train teachers and students how to prevent violence, but $0.00 to train and arm teachers. Plus, money for "anonymous" Tips about threats.

Image this. "Johnny stole Joe's girlfriend. Joe is very angry. Joe calls anonymously to report Johnny may be preparing to bomb his school. Johnny is arrested, fingerprinted, mug shot, held in jail overnight. Police get search warrant for Johnny's house. Johnny is a chemistry major and does have some chemicals in his house. Despite his impeccable reputation and being a straight A student with no record of any kind, Johnny is now charged with 'possible' intent to bomb the school, kept in jail without bond. Parents panic. Johnny now has a record which will follow him for life, while being completely innocent. All because of an anonymous phone call".

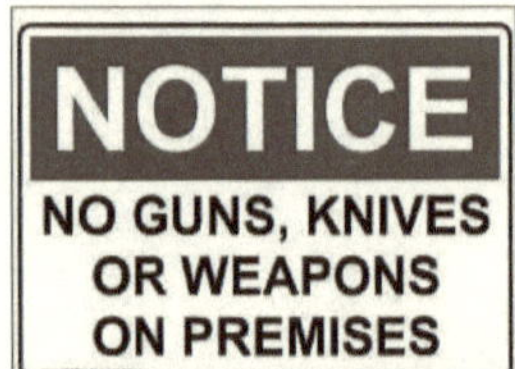

This is a simple example. Imagine where this could lead, when anyone can accuse another person of something wrong, AND DO IT ANONYMOUSLY!!!

And this sign is still prominently displayed at schools:

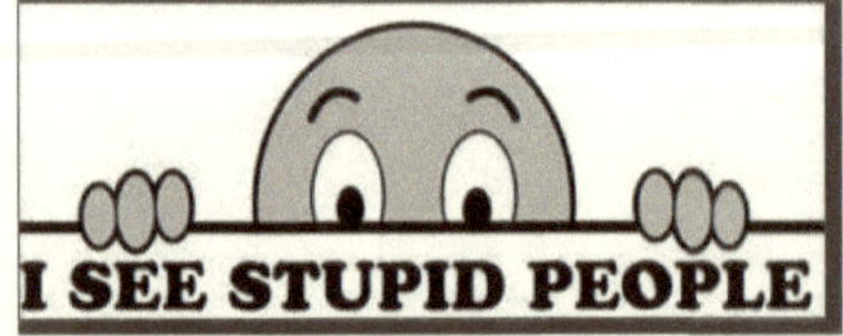

When I look at Congress
SIC 'EM DONALD!
MAGA!!!

Thought for the day March 17, 2018

Crooks?

McCabe was fired yesterday.
McCabe is a Democrat hero.

Sic 'Em Donald!

McCabe is a lying, crooked, undesirable.

Republicans are racist because they think Democrats, or anyone who breaks the law, should be punished.

Democrats who break the law, and get caught, become mortars, because they think laws don't apply to them, only other people.

"Breaking the law is my right!"

Stop a moment. Count the lying, cheating, crooked, undesirables, walking around, flaunting, what they, so far, have gotten away with.

SIC 'EM DONALD! MAGA!!!

Thought for the day March 19, 2018
SWAMPINGTON, D.C.

Like I told you last year, and the year before, and the year before, Washington, DC is full of swamp critters.

For decades they have been comfortably feathering their nest, loading their bank accounts, all at our expense. They have been caught in the trap they set for others, and they are desperately flailing away, slashing this way and that.

Anything goes.

They have been so cunning for so long, in hiding their secret money making deals while promising us prime rib and giving us, no not giving, selling us salt pork, pinto beans, and cold water cornbread, at an exorbitant price.

TRUMP HAS NOW EXPOSED THEM FOR WHAT THEY ARE. IN ONE WORD, THEY ARE CROOKS. IN 4 WORDS THEY ARE SOPHISTICATED, PROFESSIONAL, RUTHLESS, CROOKS.

So, be careful, very careful, about the propaganda garbage you swallow. Having been exposed, the squealing lies are flooding the cooperative Media. Swampington, D.C. is so bad, it is difficult to comprehend the depth of the corruption.

It is Bad, Bad.

SIC 'EM DONALD! MAGA!!!

Thought for the day March 21, 2018
WHERE DID ALL THE WOMEN GO?

Mount Holyoke College is a liberal arts college FOR women, founded in 1837, in South Hadley, Massachusetts.

Tuition $48,000

Enrollment 2300

School motto: That our daughters may be as corner stones,   polished after the similitude of a palace

BJ Melton

Recently, a <u>school produced guide</u> titled
"Supporting Transgender and Non-Binary students"
instructs professors "When addressing or 'discussing' the student body, use the word 'Student'. Do not say 'Women' ".
YOU KNEW IT WAS COMING, DIDN'T YOU?
A WOMAN'S ONLY COLLEGE WITH NO WOMEN.

CAN'T HELP BUT THINK ABOUT SODOM AND GOMORRAH.

Thanks for the day March 23, 2018

??????????
I THOUGHT this would be a good day to say thanks. The tariff deal spooked the market, and, on paper, a lot money evaporated into thin air.

But I got up this morning!

You can't put a dollar value on that.

So, I say "Thanks, Lord, for another day".
However, this picture showed up on the internet this morning.
It is interesting, but what does it mean? If you know, please tell me.
SIC 'EM DONALD! MAGA!!!

Thought for the day March 24, 2018
The fork
Sometimes I wonder about me and my thought process.

Sic 'Em Donald!

For lunch today I had leftover roast, tomatoes, and English peas. I was using my one fork to pick up everything. Peas were a problem, but I made it work.

As I stabbed my 4-tine fork into the meat, I got to wondering WHAT MAKES A FORK A FORK?

So, I did some research. Surprisingly, during the middle ages everything was eaten with a knife, a spoon, and hands. In the 16th and 17th century, a few people, mostly the elite, started using some type of fork. Then a new set of etiquette rules was developed, specifying the proper use of a fork.

Slowly over the years, the use of forks spread to the peasants. Then specialize forks were developed for specific uses; oyster forks, lobster forks, salad forks, terrapin forks, berry forks, lettuce forks, sardine forks, pickle forks, fish forks, meat forks, and pastry forks—just to name a few. Pitch forks are not used. There are 2 tine, 3 tine, 4 tine, and 5 tine forks. Plastic forks, plain metal forks, silver- and silver-plated forks.

Back to the beginning. I looked at the 4 tines on my fork.

There are no hooks, just smooth tines. So, as I stuck my fork into the meat, why did the meat stick to the fork?

Finally, in all of my research, I found no explanation of WHAT MAKES A FORK A FORK?

I did, however, learn there are specific etiquette rules for every occasion, even one where hand use is permitted.

So, to not be embarrassed, learn the rules.

Oh, and there's the napkin. What are the rules for the napkin? Now you see why we <u>both</u> wonder about me.

25 - Stormy

Thought for the day March 25, 2018
To help get your perception perfect.

SIC 'EM DONALD!

Thought for the day March 27, 2018
Guns

Last Saturday there were massive parades in the United States of America. Mostly they consisted of young people demanding our government protect them from people who want to kill people with GUNS. Without thinking, they seem to think politicians can stop the killing. Pass more laws? We got books full of laws describing the many ways a person can kill another person, and these laws prescribe an 'appropriate' punishment.

So, their warped thinking says, "Void the 2nd Amendment", which gives people the right to bear arms, to protect themselves from others who might harm them, AND THE GOVERNMENT!

Think about this panacea. The innocent has no guns. There are bad guys, and we will always have bad guys, but the government police will protect us. No worry.

Sorry, that is just a dream. No, not just a dream--a nightmare. The following quotation attributed to Hitler may or may not have been his, but it makes a point.

> This year will go down in history! For the first time, a civilized nation has full gun registration! Our streets will be safer, our police more efficient, and the world will follow our lead into the future!

After WWI Germany passed strict laws about who could buy a gun, and Jews were prohibited from purchasing one.

When Hitler and his Gestapo took power the "cleansing" of the German population began and over 6,000,000 Jews were murdered. Declining morality and desensitizing the value of human life, by killing babies through abortion, is our real problem.

Not guns. Cain killed his brother Abel, before guns. People have been killing people forever, with knives, rocks, bombs, fists, even pillows.

Yes, pillows! There is a serial killer in the Dallas area who smothers old people with a pillow.

Like I said there will always be bad guys. But putting God's moral principles back in homes, schools, government, military, courts, Congress, the FBI, AND CHURCHES, would minimize the killing.

Hopefully, the country can be retrieved from the hell hole of "do what feels good gospel" has put us in.

Taking away guns from the innocent, only gives more freedom TO THE BAD GUYS TO DO THEIR THING!

SIC 'EM DONALD!

Thought for the day March 29, 2018
Crisis

The continuing Democrat strategy- create one fake crisis after another Crooked Hillary, Crooked Hillary, Crooked Hillary, Crooked Hillary, Crooked Hillary, Crooked Hillary,

Bernie, Bernie, Bernie, Bernie, Bernie, Bernie, Pocahontas, Pocahontas, Pocahontas, Russia, Russia, Russia, Russia.

Putin, Putin, Putin, Putin, Putin, Putin,

Comey, Comey, Comey, Comey, Comey, Comey,

Mueller, Mueller, Mueller, Mueller, Mueller, Mueller, Stormy, Stormy, Stormy, Stormy, Stormy, Stormy, Care to guess what is next? Money?

SIC 'EM DONALD! MAGA!!!

Thought for the day March 30, 2018
Journalism

Stormy Daniels

Anderson Cooper and boy friend

Stormy Daniels, a "star" of many pornographic movies, was 'interviewed' Sunday night on CBS TV by openly gay Anderson Cooper, who is also a host on Clinton News Network, (CNN) 360 news.

I have to ask you, did you really expect to learn anything from a hooker, someone who has proudly become a millionaire, plying her trade, and who consistently lies, being interviewed by an extremely biased GAY Democrat, who hates Trump.

Seems to me that what is left of 'journalism' has fallen to the bottom of the cesspool.

PS: I read where Cooper and boyfriend have broken up and he is now courting someone else.

SIC 'EM DONALD! MAGA!!!

26 - Enigma

Thought for the day March 31, 2018

ANOTHER ENIGMA!

Yesterday was known as Good Friday, designated by someone, as the day of the year Jesus Christ was crucified on a cross.

In most 'Christian' countries, it is a holiday. But, not the largest "Christian' country in the world, The United States of America.

This 'Christian' nation is an enigma.

All government offices were open. Mail was delivered.

The stock market was closed.

Banks were open.

Schools were closed.

Eleven of our states take a holiday, but 39 do not.

My garbage was picked up.

Good Friday is known as a religious holiday. Atheists and our Supreme court say The First Amendment forbids the country to observe or recognize any religion.

Don't misunderstand. I am not saying Good Friday should or should not be a holiday. We know Christ was crucified on a Friday, but we do not know, for sure, the month, or day of the month.

The Resurrection was on a Sunday, the first day of the week.

We are told to celebrate the resurrection, and commune with our Lord on "Easter" Sunday and EVERY SUNDAY in the year!

Every Sunday is special.

This 'Christian' nation is an enigma.

PS: Christ had been crucified and resurrected over 1500 years, before anyone thought about 'Good Friday' and 'Easter'. Think about that.

Thought for the Day April 4, 2018

This showed up in my inbox today and I think it is worth forwarding. I know it is nothing new, but some things are good to be reminded of.

MARY'S LAMB

Mary, had a little Lamb,

His fleece was white as snow.

And everywhere that Mary went,

The Lamb was sure to go. He followed her to school each day,

T'wasn't even in the rule. It made the children laugh and play,

To have The Lamb at school.

And then the rules all changed one day,
Illegal it became;
To bring The Lamb of God to school,
Or even speak His Name!
Every day got worse and worse,
And days turned into years.
Instead of hearing children laugh,
We heard gun shots and tears.
What must we do to stop the crime,
That's in our Schools today?
Let's let The Lamb come back to school,
And teach our kids to pray!

Thought for the day April 10, 2018
Times have changed.

When I was young, growing up in the little town of Merkel, Texas, there was a boy and his mother that everybody whispered about.

You see, his mother was not married, and nobody knew who the father was. The boy was called a bastard.

Having children out of wedlock was a NO NO. People back then were very religious and on Sunday, the little town of Merkel shut down and everyone went to church.

Looking back at the way people treated the boy and his mother, I guess you would call them narrow minded.

My, how times have changed!

Today, there is a former football player, World champion wrestler, and now a millionaire movie star, called The Rock, who married his college sweetheart, and had a child. Ten years later, in 2007, after she helped make him rich, they amicably divorced.

OK. No big deal. Happens all the time. But this is a little strange. She continues to promote him, making him richer. But, in 2007, he moved in with his current 'partner' (or she moved in with him).

Today, eleven years later, they have a two year child and are expecting another.

What makes this story, somewhat, is they had planned to make the union legal this spring, BUT,

she is pregnant again AND SHE DOESN'T WANT TO GET MARRIED IN HER WHITE WEDDING GOWN WITH HER TUMMY SHOWING, so, they have postponed the wedding plans. Meanwhile, Hollywood is all agog and celebrating that one of their own, is having another child out of wedlock. I guess you call this broadminded.

TIMES HAVE CHANGED, BUT NOT FOR THE BETTER.

PS: The 'bastard' problem has been pretty much solved, by being Broadminded, and by Planned Parenthood aborting an unwanted child before they take a breath of life.

THOUGHT FOR THE DAY April 11, 2018

Another scam?

ORGANIC and GLUTEN FREE are catch words today. These words in the grocery store sell a lot of stuff at inflated prices.

I went to the store yesterday. We like bananas.

I found two different places with bananas.

One said Organic at $.79/lb.

One was just plain old, take your chances, bananas, at $.59/lb.

I ask myself 'What is the difference between an 'organic' banana and a plain old banana'? All of our bananas are grown in South America. They are harvested when still green, by people who do not speak English and can't even say 'organic'. But the owners play a game with us. Knowing some people have to have organic 'stuff' for HEALTH reasons, some are labeled Organic and demand a higher price. They are crated, put on a boat to the USA, and end up in grocery stores.

So, I ask myself, if there really are 'Organic' bananas, are they worth 20 cents more per pound? And how can I be sure one labeled 'organic' is not just a 'plain old banana'? Not by color.

All bananas look alike.

Next, I went to buy butter. I found butter for $2.69/lb. Then I noticed some other butter was labeled "Gluten Free" for $4.99/lb.!!!!!

I KNOW BUTTER IS GLUTEN FREE!!!

So, I have just concluded 'ORGANIC' and 'GLUTEN FREE' is, for the most part, a CON GAME designed to extract a little more money from uninformed customers.

27 – Concealed Carry

Thought for the day April 12, 2018

Concealed carry

Pistol-packing 'Women for Trump' graduation photo brings torrent of 'hate'!!!!
75,000 likes...75001 counting mine

Thought for the day April 13, 2018

Brenda Spencer received this response to her Graduating picture.
(likes now 120,000 and growing)

Sic 'em Brenda!
Sic 'em Alana!

'Like' count at 120,000 and climbing!

28 – Tax Day

Thought for the day April 14, 2018

Yesterday was April 13, our 21st anniversary.

It was also Friday the 13th.

All my life, I have been told Friday the 13th is a bad luck day. So, we did nothing, took no chances, NOT that we are superstitious, BUT....

Why flirt with the unknown?

Today I got to thinking about the 13th's bad name. Why?

Well, sometimes something bad happens on Friday 13, And it just reinforces our conception about it being unlucky.

<u>Assad of Syria crossed the red line... And Trump bombed him! Friday the 13th was a very bad day for him.</u>

I have learned there is a word for the number 13. It is, triskaidekaphobia and means "<u>Fear of #13</u>'. There is another word for <u>fear of "Friday the 13th"</u>, paraskevidekatriaphobia.

Where did these fears originate? Some think the 13th may be bad because there were 13, counting Jesus, at the Lord's supper, and one of them betrayed Jesus. That was really bad luck! Really, there is not a good reason, but the thought has been promoted for centuries.

So, let's face it, 13 is a bad number.

After all, names like triskaidekaphobia and paraskevidekatriaphobia deserve some respect. Just trying to pronounce them could bring trouble.

But 13 doesn't get all the bad luck. There is the Black Cat, breaking a mirror, walking under a ladder, and simply spilling a little salt.

Most hotels do not have a 13th floor.

And every morning, you have to make sure you get out bed on the same side you got in to it!

TONIGHT GIVE THANKS YOU MADE IT THROUGH THE DAY-- IF YOU DO!

THOUGHT FOR THE DAY APRIL 15, 2018

This is April 15, the famous, and dreaded IRS Day.

Taxes are due.

Since the beginning of my 'earning' life, I have filed an income tax return, and paid the taxes on my taxable income.

When I only had one income source, filing was relatively simple.

But as I got older and made some investments, life got more complicated. Then I retired with a pension, social security, and some investments. It seems the tax laws change every year, making it impossible for me to have any confidence in computing my own taxes.

So, for many years I have used a CPA who keeps up with the changing laws. Recently, a clerk for IRS audited my 2016 return, and incorrectly counted a huge loss as 'taxable' income and said I owed over $10,000 in taxes, plus interest and penalties.

I am threatened with garnishing my bank account, or selling my house, or going to jail, all unpleasant options. My CPA has written an epistle detailing why this IRS clerk is mistaken.

Hopefully, he will see the error of his ways. I am just "little" people

and easily intimidated.

Now here comes Al Sharpton, free as a bird. He has owed the IRS over $5,000,000 for years, yet he is untouched. During the Obama years, Al was a welcome guest in the White House 60-80 times.

Why hasn't he been arrested and made to pay? Yeah? Why?

Here he is, laughing and joking with Obama and good Ole Joe, without a care, and like I said, "free as a bird".

Why do our laws apply full force to a nobody like me?

BUT NOT TO "SOMEBODYS" LIKE SHARPTON AND HILLARY AND COMEY! WHY?

Thought for the day April 18, 2018

Mess

Have you noticed? This world is a mess.

Mainly, because it is full of people.

And there are so many different kinds of people. Different colors, speak different languages, have different wants and needs, believe in different things, different morals, or no morals at all, some are kind, some are cruel, some are 'smart', some are ignorant, some are healthy, many are sick-both mentally and physically, There are liars, cheats, crooks, murderers, con artists, harassers, sex crazed and promoters, There are the rich and the want to be rich, The greedy, and the power hungry. Then, there are those who "know" they are better than anyone else.

Suddenly, without my intent, we have the definition of a politician.

Fortunately, there are a lot of good people, like us, pushing back, trying to prevent being overwhelmed.
    AMEN.

Thought for the day April 20, 2018
Funny

This came in the mail today. Someone shared it with me, so, I am sharing it with you.

I took my dad to the mall the other day to buy some new shoes (he's 87). We decided to grab a bite at the food court. I noticed he was

watching a teenager sitting next to him. The teenager had spiked hair in all different colors - green, red, orange, and blue.

My dad kept staring at her. The teenager kept looking and would find my dad staring every time. When the teenager had enough, she sarcastically asked: "What's the matter old man, never done anything wild in your life?"

Knowing my Dad, I quickly swallowed my food so that I would not choke on his response; I knew he would have a good one! In classic style he responded without batting an eyelid

"Got stoned once and had sex with a parrot. I was just wondering if you're my kid."

Thought for the day April 21, 2018
Just thinking

It is not your fault you were born.
It is not your fault you are male/female.
It is not your fault you are black, white, brown, or yellow.
You are what you are and not by choice.
You will live until you die.
WHAT HAPPENS IN BETWEEN IS YOUR FAULT. THINK ABOUT IT.

29 – Swamp Critters

LONG! Thought for the day April 23, 2018
Corruption in DC? Some swamp critters.

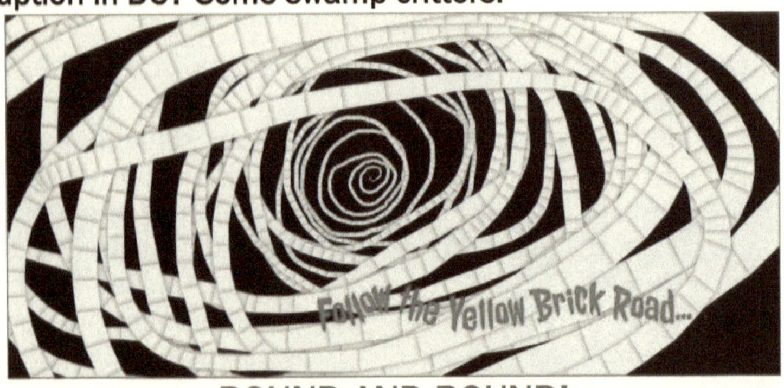

ROUND AND ROUND!

From 2001 to 2005, they were investigating the Clinton Foundation.

A Grand Jury was empaneled.

World Governments donated to the "Charity".

2001 to 2003 no "Donations" to the Clinton Foundation were declared.

Now, that's interesting, isn't it?

Who took over this investigation in 2002? James Comey.

Now, that's interesting, isn't it?

Guess who was transferred in to the Internal Revenue Service to run the Tax Exemption Branch of the IRS? Your friend and mine, Lois Lerner, the denier of tax exemption to conservative groups.

Now, that's interesting, isn't it?

Guess who ran the Tax Division inside the Department of Injustice from 2001 to 2005?

Assistant Attorney General of the United States, Rod Rosenstein.

Now, that's interesting, isn't it?

Guess who was the Director of the Federal Bureau of Investigation during this timeframe???

Incredible coincidence, Robert Mueller.

Comey, Lerner, Rosenstein, Mueller

What do all four of these characters have in common?

They were front line investigators into the Clinton Foundation Investigation.

Let's fast forward to 2009.

Sic 'Em Donald!

James Comey leaves the Justice Department to go and cash-in at Lockheed Martin. (This is a story in itself) Hillary Clinton is running the State Department, using personal email server.

Hillary learns of the Uranium One "issue".

Looking out for America's best interest, she approves the sale of 20% of US Uranium to no other than, the Russians! Good deal, you say?

America got absolutely nothing out of it.

However, prior to the sales approval, no other than Bill Clinton goes to Moscow, gets paid 500K for a one-hour speech then meets with Vladimir Putin at his home for a few hours.

Interesting? Ok, no big deal, right?

Well, not so fast, the FBI had a mole inside the money laundering and bribery scheme.

Guess who was the FBI Director during this timeframe?

Yep, Robert Mueller. He even delivered, <u>secretly</u>, on September 21, 2009, a highly enriched Uranium Sample to <u>Georgia Tbilisi</u> | <u>Russia Moscow</u>,

ON ORDERS OF OUR Secretary of state, Hillary Clinton.

Guess who was handling that case within the Justice Department out of the US Attorney's Office in Maryland. No other than, Rod Rosenstein.

Guess what happened to the informant who made this public. The Department of Justice placed a GAG order on him and threatened to lock him up if he spoke out about it. How does 20% of the most strategic asset of the United States of America end up in Russian hands when the FBI has an informant, a mole providing inside information to the FBI on the criminal enterprise?

Guess what happened soon after the sale was approved? ~145 million dollars in "donations" made their way into the Clinton Foundation from entities directly connected to the Uranium One deal.

Guess who was still at the Internal Revenue Service working the Charitable Division? No other than, Lois Lerner. Ok, that's all just another series of coincidences, nothing to see here, right? Let's fast forward to 2015.

Due to a series of tragic events in Benghazi and after 9

"investigations" by the House, Senate and at State Department, Trey Gowdy, running the 10th investigation, as Chairman of the Select Committee on Benghazi, discovers that Hillary ran the State Department on an

<u>unclassified, unauthorized, outlaw personal email server.</u> He also discovered that none of those emails had been turned over when she departed her "Public Service" as Secretary of State which was required by law.

He also discovered that there was <u>Top Secret information</u> contained within her personally archived email.

Sparing you the State Departments cover up, the nostrums they floated, the delay tactics that were employed and the

outright lies that were spewed forth from the necks of the Kerry State Department, we shall leave it with this...... they did everything humanly possible to cover for Hillary.

Now this is amazing. Guess who became FBI Director in 2013?

JAMES COMEY, BACK FROM Lockheed!

How interesting!

Guess who secured 17 no bid contracts for his employer (Lockheed Martin) with the State Department and was rewarded with a six million dollar thank you present when he departed his employer. No other than James Comey.

Amazing how all those no-bids just went right through at State, huh?

How interesting.

Now he is the FBI Director in charge of the "Clinton Email Investigation" after, of course, his FBI Investigates the Lois Lerner "Matter" at the Internal Revenue Service and <u>exonerates her.</u>

Nope couldn't find any crimes there.

Can you guess what happened next?

In April 2016, James Comey drafts an exoneration letter of Hillary Rodham Clinton. Meanwhile the DOJ is handing out immunity deals like candy. They didn't even convene a Grand Jury.

Like a lightning bolt of statistical impossibility, like a miracle from God himself, like the true "Gangsta" Comey is, James steps out into the cameras of an awaiting press conference on July the 8th of 2016 and exonerates Hillary from any wrongdoing. Can you see the pattern? It goes on and on, Rosenstein becomes Asst. Attorney General,

Comey gets fired based upon a letter by Rosenstein, Comey leaks government information to the press, <u>Mueller is assigned to the Russian Investigation sham by Rosenstein to provide cover for decades of malfeasance within the FBI and DOJ and the story continues.</u> The coincidentalist coincidence of all coincidences.

<u>Former FBI Director Robert Mueller won plaudits from both sides of the aisle for being named by the Department of Justice to serve as special counsel to investigate allegations of Russian interference in the 2016 election and rumors of collusion between Russia and the Trump campaign.</u> <u>Will coincidences never cease?</u>

THE FOX IS NOW GUARDING THE HEN HOUSE.

Thought for the day April 24, 2018

FISA Abuse, political espionage.... pick a crime, any crime, chances are...... this group and a few others did it.

All the same players. All compromised and conflicted.

All working fervently to NOT go to jail themselves.

All connected in one way or another to the Clinton's. They are like battery acid, they corrode and corrupt everything they touch.

How many lives have these two destroyed? The Clinton Foundation, in its 20+ years

of operation of being the largest International Charity Fraud in the history of mankind, has never been audited by the Internal Revenue Service.

Coincidentally, Comey's brother works for DLA Piper, the law firm that does the Clinton Foundation's taxes.

How interesting.

My 'interest' cup over flows!

SIC 'EM DONALD!!

Thought for the day May 1, 2018

At home with royalty

This photograph is being circulated with Reagan's 'supposed' quotation:

"For the life of me. And I'll never know how to explain it, When I met that young man, I felt like I was the one Shaking hands with a President."

It is not true. Nobody knows what their exchange was.

It is just unnecessary FAKE news. BUT it does show that even at age 40, Donald was at home with Royalty!

SIC 'EM DONALD! MAGA!!!

2nd Thought for May 1, 2018
Class act

Saturday night, April 28, 2018, at the so-called Correspondents Dinner, this lady, Sarah Sanders, while being decimated, castigated, derided, ridiculed, and called a liar, demonstrated what true class is----- while sitting just 8 feet away from the foul-mouthed comedian. (I use the term extremely loosely).

It was a classic demonstration of how HATE has filled the bowels of the MEDIA.

SIC 'EM SARAH!

30 – Deep State

Thought for the day May 2, 2018 Joined **at the hip**
If you care about America, if you care about

President Trump, if you care about yourself and your family, this might interest you.

After 9/11, we went crazy. A thousand or more people, supposedly terrorists, were arrested and jailed without being formally charged (some for months, some still in Guantanamo). The Bush administration began gathering "intelligence" proving Iraq was responsible and Saddam was developing Weapons of Mass Destruction. When enough information was gathered, they "proved" to us, the American people, that war was justified, and away we went!

Involved in this scheme were two names that have now become very familiar-Robert Mueller and James Comey—who today are reported to be "joined at the hip". Desperate for creditable information, torture programs were set up and approved for CIA. Agents were simply instructed not to document such torture, (Remember Waterboarding?) and any "war crimes files" were made to disappear. Not only did "collect it all" illegal surveillance and torture programs continue, but Mueller's (and then Comey's) FBI later worked to prosecute NSA and CIA whistleblowers who revealed these illegalities.

Neither Comey nor Mueller deserve their current lionization among politicians and mainstream media. These two close collaborators, "joined at the hip" merely proved themselves, along with former CIA Director George "Slam Dunk" Tenet, to be political crooks, absorbed in their power to prosecute, and punish the innocent and the guilty. Justice be damned! This "partnership" of Mueller-Comey, is said to be "one of the closest working relationships the top ranks of the Justice Department have ever seen, "Mueller was chosen as <u>Special Counsel</u>, not because he has integrity,

BECAUSE HE HAS NONE, but because he will do what the powerful want him to do. He didn't speak the truth about the Iraq war he knew to be unjustified.

He didn't speak out against torture. He didn't speak out against unconstitutional surveillance. And he didn't tell the truth about 9/11. He is just the SWAMP'S MAN. He will do what the powerful want him to do. His mission DESTROY TRUMP!

ANY MISSTEP, A STRAW, A SLIP OF THE LIP, WILL DO.

Thought for the Day May 3, 2018
Destruction

Michael Caputo, Broken and Broke

Grilled unmercifully Wednesday for 3 hours by Mueller lawyers, Caputo reached the boiling point.

Former Trump campaign adviser Michael Caputo says he has spent $125,000 on lawyers to comply with the demands of the Senate Intelligence Committee, more than he makes in a year. Wednesday, he exploded, with understandable profanity, at Democratic Senate aides after he loses his house to legal fees in 'witch hunt' congressional Russia probe. 'I want to know who cost us so much money, who crushed our kids, who forced us out of our home, all because you lost an election,' he told Democrats.

Why? You know why!
It is Destroy Trump!
Destroy his family!
Destroy his friends!
Destroy his businesses!
Destroy the Republican party!
Vicious! All to save the SWAMP!

HANG TOUGH, DONALD! BE SMART!

Thought for the day May 6, 2018

On May 2, 2018 I mentioned Mueller and Comey being "joined at the hip". This is a correction. Research has determined that Obama, Mueller, and Comey were "joined at the hip".

Research also reveals many almost unbelievable things about the DEEP STATE.

More later.

SIC 'EM DONALD! WATCH YOUR BACK!!!

Thought for the day May 10, 2018
Deep state #2

Did you know John Kerry served in Vietnam for 4 months? Did you know he got 3 purple hearts for a hang nail, an arm scratch, and a minor shrapnel wound, yet never missed any duty time?

Did you know He was awarded the Bronze star and Silver Star, for unmercifully attacking and destroying small Vietnam villages and fishing boats?

Did you know he came home and gave an interview to Congress describing in minute detail the horrors of wars and desecrating American soldiers for similar atrocities?

He then protested the war and apparently threw his ribbons and medals away. He has denied this many times since, but never produced physical evidence of the metals. He became a Democrat Senator from Massachusetts, married a billionaire, ran for President as a Democrat in 2004, was named Obama's Secretary of State in 2013, succeeding her Highness, Hillary Clinton.

As Secretary of State, he pushed Obama's "Agreement" with Iran, giving Iran $150 billion not build a nuclear weapon for seven years, while Iranians were in the street yelling "Death to America"!

What a friend!

Today, the treasonous John Kerry has failed in his efforts to preserve the 'Agreement'.

Obama's last "legacy" has disappeared. President Trump, as promised, cut off both his legs, and withdrew from the disastrous "Agreement".

The Deep State took a lick!

SIC 'EM DONALD!

Thought for the day May 12, 2018
Deep State# 3

Yesterday President Trump announced the beginning of his war on DRUG PRICES.

Think about this.

Hillary Clinton, in 2013, after filling the coffers of the Clinton Foundation with bribe money from Foreign Muslim countries, resigned as Secretary of State, and started preparing to be President of the United states, a role she had "rightfully earned".

Assured of this "inevitable" occurrence, the DRUG Industry began their "non-Government interference Campaign" by bribing Her Highness. In 2014, the Drug Industry ~~paid~~ bribed her to give

115

5 speeches, <u>giving her $1,200,000 (that's million)</u>

Talk about <u>blood</u> money

These mammoth drug organizations

(Biotech Industry Organization, Pharmaceutical Care Management Association.

Drug Chemical & Associated Technologies. Advanced Medical Technology

Association,

Novo Nordisk, the $130 billion Big Pharma) Paid her as follows:

February 2014 - paid Hillary $125,000

March 2014, she received $250,000 On March 13th, 2014 She was paid $225,000 in June 2014 Her compensation: $335,000 In October 2014, collected a quick $265,000 <u>Repeat $1,200,000!</u>

If she had been elected, you would never have seen this:

Yesterday President Trump announced the beginning of his war on DRUG PRICES.

Another lick for the Deep State!

SIC ' DONALD!!!

Thought for the day May 15, 2018
Deep State # 4

The Vietnam War was in the 1960's. Many of you were not alive then.

A draft was instituted, and young men were drafted into the army and sent to Vietnam. (My son, Rick, was one of them) Bill Clinton was drafted, given a serial number 3 26 46 228, classified 1-A and ordered to report.

He ignored the order.

He then used various angles to avoid being in the army.

He joined a protest group in the early '70's.

He was a guilty felon.

Jimmy Carter pardoned him in 1978.

He became a lawyer and then Governor of Arkansas.

He married his mistress, Hillary, and she became FLO Arkansas. It is not known, for sure, if Hillary turned frigid, or if Bill just had an insatiable appetite for women.

Bill got in much trouble with several women, which cost him much money.

It was all poo pooed, denied, and swept under the rug. Bill became President, a pardoned FELON for dodging the draft, and he is now Commander in Chief of all of our military, and Hillary is FLOTUS, and hates the military!

Sic 'Em Donald!

Trouble followed him and he was impeached for lying under oath. But Congress forgave him, and he retired with a President's salary for life. Not the end of the story.

Hillary was first 'Lady" of Arkansas, and First Lady of the United States. She now has a resume. New York elected her Senator. Then Obama made her Secretary of State.

Now her resume includes being the worst Secretary of State, EVER! Resume is growing, now qualified, without question, to be President.

Has "earned" the right to be President!

Donald Trump stomped on her resume.

A BIG LICK ON THE DEEP STATE!
SIC 'EM DONALD!!!

31 - Mueller

Thought for the day May 17, 2018
Deep State # 5

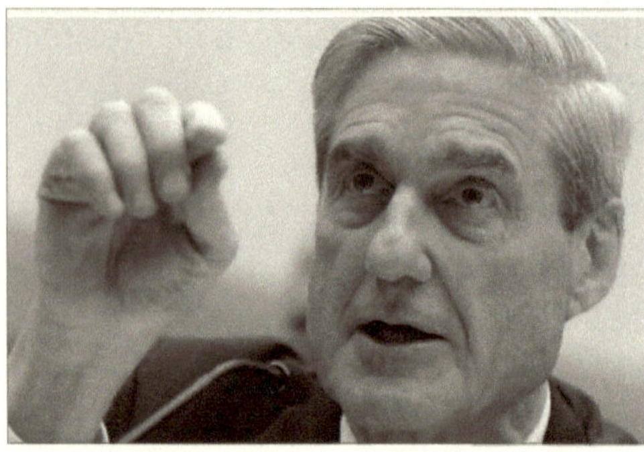

Robert Mueller, assassin

This man is not a Christian.

This man was head of the FBI 2001-2013.

This man, under Bush and Obama, oversaw the Deep State corruption of the FBI AND THE DOJ.

This man was once a patriot.

Today, he is an unscrupulous, greedy 'person', who has had a taste of blood, and now his appetite for more blood is insatiable.

He sold his soul to the Deep State years ago.

Put your thumb on him, Donald!!!

KILLING DEEP STATE ONE AT A TIME.

Thought for the Day May 21, 2018
Deep State # 6

Garbage. We are swimming in it.

Here are the news items for today.

? Peace? with North Korea?

Trading with cheating China.

Trading with Mexico.

The WALL.

NATO and their "friend" Iran.

A fantasy 'Royal Wedding'.

Putin.

Parasite Mueller and his 17 prosecuting lawyers.

School shootings.

Gun "Control"

Immigration.

Crooks in the FBI and DOJ and the IRS.

Crooks in Congress.

Harassment!

Sic 'Em Donald!

Then there is Jeff Sessions, our Attorney General, the most powerful policeman in the United States, The protector of our Freedom, The enforcer of our laws.

Sorry, I said there is Jeff Sessions, anomaly.

WHERE IS Jeff Sessions?

From here he looks like a nothing, doing nothing.

Has the Deep State got control of him? Apparently. Donald!!! Flush the toilet!! Fire this incompetent so-and-so before he lets the house burn down!

SIC 'EM DONALD!!!

Thought for the day May 26, 2018
MEMORIAL DAY

Today is Saturday, the beginning of the weekend most Americans pause to remember, and honor, those who have served and those who have died for our freedom. All over Richardson and the USA our flag is flying.

For many it is a sad day. Beautiful memories of loved ones we have lost, race through our mind and we shed a tear, grateful that someone we loved, and millions we never knew, gave their life so we can live free and unafraid.

THEN I REMEMBER JESUS CHRIST. HE DIED FOR ME, TOO!

Thought for the day May 28, 2018
S h i f t y

I can't figure this guy. I think his birth name was Schiffty, but he got so much bullying in school, he dropped the ty. It did not change his character or make him any friends.

So he moved to California where he found clones just like him.

But a bitter childhood left him with a warped mind, and full of hate. He, now, supposedly, represents some of his constituents in Congress, but mainly, he represents himself.

Some have suggested he is eyeing running for

President as an ultra-liberal, far, far left Democrat in 2020.

If so, he is burning bridges that can't be repaired.
Hate has destroyed many people.

Some of this may be Fake news, but not all.

SIC 'EM DONALD!!! MAGA!!!

32 - Normandy

THOUGHT FOR THE DAY MAY 29, 2018
Something you may not know.

Normandy, France... A total of 9387 Americans buried here

There are 17 cemeteries scattered over Europe and England where American military personnel are buried, Heroes who died to save Europe and England from itself.

Each burial site is marked with a cross. The grounds are perpetually maintained, immaculately. Our flag flies over this hallowed ground.

I was once privileged to visit Normandy Beach and this cemetery.

I stood by this statue and gazed at the thousands of crosses.

You can't help but feel a sense of pride and gratefulness. But at the same time, there is sadness, sadness that so many thousands of Americans died for freedom in a foreign land and are buried in a foreign land!

Yesterday was Memorial Day, a day set aside to remember these, and many thousands more.

It is a good thing, but unfortunately, only 1% of us who has served, or suffered a loss, or somehow come to realize the COST of freedom.

In the other 99%, there are a few who desecrate or disrespect our flag. They turn my stomach!

SIC 'EM DONALD!!

Thought for the day May 30, 2018
Today I sit here wondering, or maybe I am wandering.

I have had this thought before:

What is a democrat?

Then I think '"Could I be a democrat?" I look around.

I see Nancy Pelosi. She claims to be a democrat. She wants to raise my taxes, open the flood gates for immigrants of all kind to pour in to the United States, she is pro-choice. i.e.: kill dem babies.

She is 'for' everything I am against. Could we be friends?

I don't think so.

Then I see Chuck 'the Clown' Schumer, and Maxine Waters, and Dianne Feinstein. They claim to be democrats.

They think like Pelosi.

Do the masses that claim to be democrat think like this?

Hopefully not, BUT......... come November, we will see.

I could never be a democrat!

SIC 'EM DONALD!

Thought for the day June 2, 2018

Hate

Two little boys talking:

" I hate you!"

"I hate you more!"

"I double hate you!"

"I double-double hate you!"

"Nobody could hate more than I hate you!"

"I can! I just hate you more and more and more!" Interesting. Where did they learn to hate?

Probably from their parents or other adults.

Hate is a favorite pastime of grown up kids.

Hate is a bad thing. It causes fights, divorces, lost friendships, killings, wars.

Hate is a common emotion of humans. No good comes from hate.

In the bible we learn that Cain hated his brother, Abel, so he killed him.

The same bible also teaches us to 'love our neighbor'.

So, hate is bad. Love is good.

During the Presidential campaign, Hillary's supporters carried signs saying, "LOVE NOT HATE".

On the night of November 8, 2016, this huge arena was filled with thousands of people, in love with Hillary, waiting for the guaranteed 'coronation' of her highness.

Love abounded. The glass ceiling was in place.

Sic 'Em Donald!

The harbor was filled with boats full of fireworks ready to explode. As the votes were counted, everyone waited with bated breath for the official crowning.

Love was everywhere. Hate was nowhere.

Suddenly, about 3 AM on November 9, in the blink of an eye, Love was nowhere. Hate was everywhere.

Poor Hillary struck out.

There was cursing and gnashing of teeth.

And, sadly, today we have grown up children in America, hating like no one has ever hated before!

SIC 'EM DONALD!!

Thought for the day June 5, 2018
The Supreme Court and other courts.

If you have been to court, any court, the following will be somewhat familiar.

These thrones are where our nine Supreme Court Justices sit when in session. After coffee, and dressing in their long black regal robes, and at the appointed time, they march in and take their appointed throne, with the Chief taking the middle throne.

Just prior to them making their entrance, the court Bailiff shouts: ALL RISE! Everyone stands out of respect until all are seated and they have assumed their solemn, dignified, intelligent pose. Then all may sit.

Deliberations begin. In time, (usually much time, like, maybe months), decisions are made.

I think about this. Over the years, millions of decisions have been made that affect all of today. Most recently they made one which had been hanging since 2016-<u>the one about the cake baker</u>, by a 7-2 vote. May have been a good decision.

But supreme intellect Nancy Pelosi thinks the Majority got it wrong!!! (She carries her "stupids" on the tip of her tongue)

Other rulings that have gotten stuck in my craw, mainly revolve around the flag and National Anthem.

It is OK to kneel, raise your fist in defiance, or stay in the locker room, during the playing of ♫"O, say can you see...♫. It is ok to burn,

123

stomp on, or pee on our flag- freedom of expression you know. And as Obama said, saluting the flag might hurt someone's feelings, so he did no salute, even when past protocol required a salute. Which gets me to this. The same Supreme Court, which has made these detrimental rulings about the flag and Anthem, <u>require that you to stand</u> as they make their pompous self to their thrones. Kneeling would get you thrown out of court.

SIC 'EM DONALD!!!

33 – Things I worry About

Thought for the day June 6, 2018

Things I worry about
1. My next meal
2. Mowing my grass

Things President Trump worries about **EVERYDAY!**
1. United' States of America
2. North Korea
3. Mueller "investigation"
4. Attorney General Sessions
5. Iran
6. NATO
7. G7 summit
8. Inspector General report
9. Insults to family
10. Liars in FBI
11. Liars in DOJ 11. The WALL
12. Immigration
13. Trade imbalances
14. China
15. Mexico
16. Obama shadow government
17. Mid-term elections
18. Rinos in congress
19. Gun control
20. 1st Amendment
21. 2nd Amendment
22. NAFTA
23. "Friends"?
24. ISIS
25. Putin
26. Assad
27. England, Germany, France
28. California

SIC 'EM DONALD!!

Thought for the day June 7, 2018
Something stupid

Some days I have a thought and I don't know where it comes from. It is what it is.

This was, is, one of those days

Suddenly I am looking at the face of Nancy Pelosi.

Everybody knows she is a bimbo (except Her).

Many things she says are just off the wall.

No connection to reality.

This showed up in my in box today, and Nancy it the apparent author.

"I propose a limitation be put on how many squares of toilet paper can be used in any one sitting.

Now, I don't want to rob any law-abiding American of his or her God-given rights, but I think we are an industrious enough people that we can make it work with only one square per restroom visit, except, of course, on those pesky occasions where 2 to 3 could be required." –

And she thinks I am nuts!

SIC 'EM DONALD!!!

Thought for the day June 11, 2018
TONY AWARDS

If you missed the Tony Awards last night, give thanks.

I missed it-on purpose-but I read about it this morning.

Hate was prevalent in all of it 'glory'.

Because of us, these 'people' have become rich pretending to be somebody they are not, mouthing words someone told them to utter.

They are actors, not real people.

They demonstrate, through words of their own, how being rich, <u>by osmosis, they become wise and intellectually superior to the rest of us.</u> But when their 'wisdom' does not provide suitable words to describe an occasion, they substitute vulgarity and profanity. So, the Tony's last night was all about aggrandizing people who hate people like you and me, President Trump, and America. They glory in sex, promiscuity, and love the Harvey Weinstein's so prevalent in Hollywood.

THEY LOVE ONE ANOTHER. HATE ANY OTHER. SICK.

Thought for the day June 12, 2018

Hate - Digging for dirt!

MSNBC anchor Stephanie Ruhle mocked <u>President Trump</u> on his preparation for an upcoming summit with North Korea, asking if preparation occurred

"when you appeared in a Playboy soft-core porn movie" during her mid-morning newscast on Friday.

Pride

SIC 'EM DONALD!!!

Thought for the day June 13, 2018
Finally LEGITIMATE!

You knew how the liberal media would spin the Trump-Kim meeting. Clinton, Bush, Obama, were all conned by North Korea promises.

Our "illegitimate" President was sure to suffer the same fate!! Poor Donald!

So here is a Chuck "The Clown" Schumer quote: <u>"Trump gave Kim what he wanted: legitimizing him by appearing next to him on the world stage."</u>

Bless the media! They are so laughable sometimes. Think about this.

Since election day November 8, 2016, Obama, George Soros, the Democrat Party, New York times and all the media have been trying to prove President Trump is our 'illegitimate' President.

Now they think he is so legitimate, he can legitimize a tyrant dictator just by being in the proximity of Kim Jong Un.

BJ Melton

The unlearned, because of their stupidity, plus their HATE for Donald, think he got snookered. Gave away the store. Conned by Kim. Here is my analysis of what I think happened.

To me, Trump has all the ego he needs.

But Kim, a 34-year-old, spoiled brat, has been cornered like a rat, and capable of doing stupid things.

A rat, when cornered or caged will fight for its life.

With a few choice words, and a handshake, Trump turned Kim into a Mickey Mouse, when he gave Kim an Ego builder:

<u>Trump said, "Mr. Chairman, it's a great honor to be with you, and I know that we will have tremendous success together."</u> So, as Mickey once said:

"The future will be a daily trudge if you keep looking back and focusing on past mistakes.

Learn and leave it in the past."

MOVE ON!
SIC 'EM DONALD!!

34 – RINOs

Thought for the day June 19, 2018
Rino Paul Ryan

A disgusting individual!

In my book "My America is Back" on page 81, written March 10, 2016, we first learned about, what we now know as, the DEEP STATE.

On that date, Millionaires and Billionaires such as Apple and Google CEO's, convened on a private island off the coast of Georgia.

Included in the group were Rinos Paul Ryan and Senate majority leader Mitch McConnell.

Reason for the meeting: STOP TRUMP! A plan was developed and $millions were donated to the "cause"!

(Rino Ryan is also mentioned negatively on pages 104, 120, 121, 123, 125 of *My America is Back*)

Obviously, the initial goal 'STOP TRUMP' failed.

It was, and is, also obvious that Ryan hates Trump. It is now 2 years since the STOP TRUMP meeting, and two-faced, forked tongue Rino Ryan, as Speaker of the House, continues to try to destroy President Trump and his program to Make America Great Again.

We need the WALL. He has sabotaged every effort to fund it.

He has stopped every attempt to solve the immigration problem.

Today he has developed his own Immigration plan, which the DEEP STATE wants, and he hopes to push it through Congress.

If passed, it will only mitigate the problem.

NOT solve it. Trump will veto it.

The liberals will then accuse him of being inhumane, coldhearted, cruel, barbaric, hateful. These are all adjectives which describe Ryan, the Deep State swamp critters, and the "Tolerate" intolerant Liberal Democrats. Plus, Ryan is a contemptible hypocrite.

SIC 'EM DONALD!!!

35 – The Great Divide

Thought for the day June 21, 2018
Hard to believe!

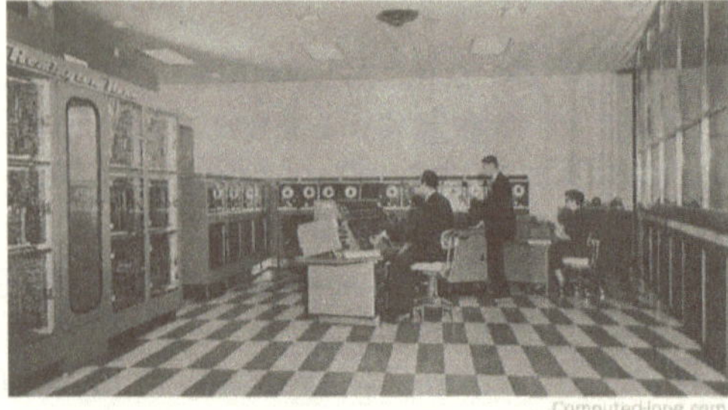

The computer in 1951!

The UNIVAC is an electrical computer containing thousands of vacuum tubes that utilizes punch cards and switches for inputting data and punch cards for outputting and storing data.

The UNIVAC was later released as the UNIVAC II, and III.

Many of these models were only owned by a few companies or government agencies.

In the above picture is an example of the UNIVAC computer.

As can be seen in the picture, this is a room-sized computer and often required multiple people to operate. Electricity cost for operating and COOLING was $thousands per month.

Today, this device, which you hold in your hand, with the touch of a button,

YOU can.... talk to similar devices-anywhere in the world! send and receive messages, take, send, and print color pictures, store tons of data, retrieve billions of bits of data watch live events real time, make movies, watch movies, make complicated calculations, buy and pay for anything on line, even a Lexus!

Pay bills Make deposits THE LIST GOES ON AND ON! Electricity cost $nil...

IMAGINE WHAT IT WILL BE LIKE IN 2050!!!

Thought for the day June 22, 2018
Photo shopping and the disgusting Media

The first picture seems to show a little boy in a cage.

It was sent worldwide by social media as an example Of Trump's cruel, heartless, callous, attitude of separating children from illegal immigrant parents.

Sad, isn't it? Yes! IF it were true!!!

Sic 'Em Donald!

Actually, the little boy was looking <u>INTO</u> a cage set up at Dallas City Hall on June 10, by Liberal "do gooders" to <u>protest Trump enforcing Obama's rules.</u> The second photo shows the little boy running free. The third photo shows the cage set up at City Hall with <u>kids laughing and giggling</u>, holding their home-made signs. I wonder where did the signs came from?

THE ULTIMATE IN FAKE NEWS.

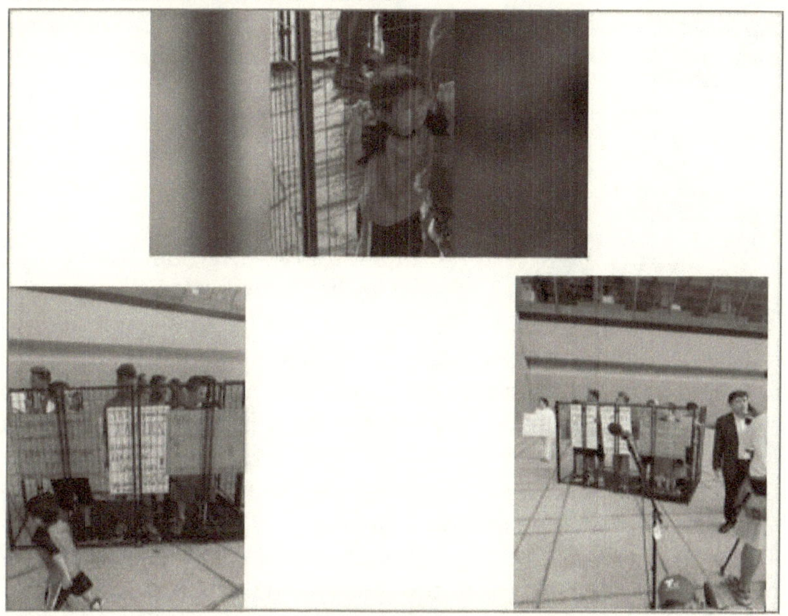

SIC 'EM DONALD!!!

Thought for the day June 25, 2018
The great divide!

America is split apart. Hatred is consuming us.

Why did this happen?

I got to thinking and for some reason I thought of Judas Iscariot.

Do you remember Judas?

When Christ began his ministry, he picked 12 apostles to help him spread the news. One of them was Judas.

Judas was picked to be the treasurer for the group. During the 3+ years he followed Jesus, supposedly learning the gospel message, he developed a love for money. Actually, he became greedy. Along came Christ's left-wing hate group of the day. They offered Judas 30 pieces of silver to point out Jesus so he could be arrested. Wow, he said, I would be rich.

Greed got him. Christ was captured, and crucified.

Christ had a message to save mankind.

Today, Trump has a message to save America from itself. The Power Hungary Greedy left-wing group of today, has developed an intense hate for Trump because he is a threat to their power AND pocketbook!!

They have sworn to destroy him! Hate has consumed them. If Trump does something Clinton, Bush, or Obama did, that they loved, they hate Trump, for whatever.

If it is good for America, the haters hate Trump!

"Crucify Trump" they scream!

So far, President Trump has survived.

Is there SOLUTION to this hate thing? I am not wise enough to know.

But I feel like a lot of people are going to be hurt really bad.

Strange. Before the election, they preached LOVE-NOT HATE.

Overnight the Lovers converted to Haters.

Thought for the day June 27, 2018
THE "BAN"

The "BAN" of Immigrants from certain Muslim dominated countries (9/11) has created cries of anguish from the 'hate America' liberals. "It's hateful, Unamerican, cruel, etc." (9/11)

Sic 'Em Donald!

There are horror stories like the one about the Muslim engineer, born in the USA, raised in Yemen, married to a Yemen woman, (9/11), who lives in Yemen with their three Yemeni children, ages 3,9,13. He has lived and worked in the USA for years, separated from his family. (9/11)

Why did he leave them in Yemen all these years?

Now his wife and children are crying "We want Daddy".

Obama would have welcomed them at the airport. (9/11)

Why, now, is he so demanding to be able to reunite with his Family?

Another Muslim American has a 16-year-old son somewhere in the Muslim world that he wants to bring to America. (9/11) Why are they separated? Where is the boy's mother? Now the boy is crying "Daddy, don't leave me in this place!" There will be more unpleasant stories.

The Hate America liberals will have protests in the streets, (9/11) with their Professionally made Hate signs, shouting gutter profanity, all promoted, and paid for, by Obama and his 'friend' George Soros.

You will note how I dropped (9/11) in here and there.

Lest we forget!

The BAN is against countries known to foster terrorism, and export terrorists.

Terrorists flew planes into the Twin towers, (9/11) killing thousands of Americans.

Terrorists world-wide have killed and mutilated many more thousands.

Muslim terrorists have taken an oath to 'Kill, kill, Americans'.

We know not all Muslims are terrorists, but all terrorist are Muslim.

The Ban is designed to keep terrorists out of America. (9/11)

"Why, Hate America Liberals, IS THAT a bad thing?"

SIC 'EM DONALD!!!

THOUGHT FOR THE DAY JUNE 28, 2018
THE SICKNESS OF HATE!

There are such lies and deception going on! Fake news abounds that tears at you heart. AND BY DESIGN!!!!

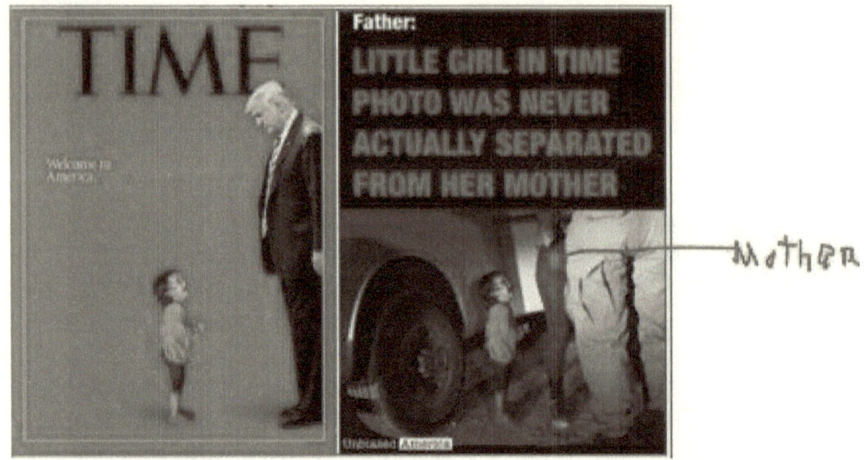

Time Magazine, first published in 1923, is now published worldwide, with an estimated readership in the USA, alone, of 20,000,000. Worldwide? Who knows?

The magazine has now become the promoter of Communism and Socialism in

America, Europe, Asia, Australia, and Middle East. It is now anti-America to the core. Maybe it always has been. Time has a reputation of selecting, and promoting, "Person of the Year".

In 1938 it was that adored dictator Adolf Hitler. In 1939 it was another mass murderer, Josef Stalin.

In 2015, Bruce Jenner, the ALL-AMERICAN Wheaties boy, was selected "Woman of the Year".

Last month, this Photo-shopped picture of Trump and the little girl was sent around the world.

Think about this. What opinions of Trump and America were formed in the minds of the 'unlearned'? None were good.

Part of the article narrative is as follows:

" In mere weeks, over 2,000 children were taken from their parents and held, alone, sometimes behind chain-link fences, under the cold care of the federal government.

In Texas, three "tender age" centers were set up for detained toddlers and infants. Incessant wails of "Mamá" and "Papá" were heard on audio from a Customs and Border Protection detention center. An advocate told of a child being led away from her mother crying so hard she vomited."

Notice the use of selected words and phrases, designed to tear at your heart strings, and, they hope, make you hate America and Trump.

SIC 'EM DONALD!!! DON'T DESPAIR!!

36 – More Maxine

Thought for the day June 29, 2018
Maxine Waters

Who is Maxine Waters? Maxine is a Representative in Congress from the California 43rd district. But she does not live in her district, which is a gang infested, poverty-stricken area of Los Angeles. Instead, she lives several miles away in a wealthy, mostly white, neighborhood. Her manor is valued at over $3,000,000, bought and paid for by taxpayers and lobbyists. Recently, she has spent very little time representing the 43rd District in Washington, DC.

She now flits around the country, speaking at protests, ranting and raving, mainly against President Trump. For months she has screeched "Impeach Trump" and recently she said she was 'going to take out Trump'.

What does that mean?

Maxine will be 80 in August. She appears and sounds like she has become completely unhinged!

But maybe it is not that at all. You have to know flitting around the country like she has been, is expensive. AND you have to know Maxine ain't paying for it, plus her Congressional Pay just goes in the bank! Obama said he was going to fight for his 'legacy', and he is- organizing riots and protests against Trump. In my logically thinking way, it becomes apparent that Obama has his hooks in Maxine and is footing her bill, plus a 'few' $$$$ on the side.

Finally, we know liars lie to cover lies. Yesterday, she announced cancellation of two protests, one in Alabama and one in Texas. Why? Supposedly she received threats of harm.

Did she, or didn't she? Maybe it was part of the 'plan'.

SIC 'HER DONALD!!!

Thought for the day July 1, 2018
Obama's Plan

You must wonder why there so many protests are going on.

Well, wonder no more. IT IS THE OBAMA PLAN.

(READ page 356 of my book MY AMERICA IS BACK) Obama, Soros, and his Moveon.org, are putting their nationwide organization of

30,000 plus protesters to work. Protesters, with paid benefits, such as health care, vacations, and bonuses, are paid "good" money to go wherever, organize protests, recruit protesters, provide professionally made signs, transportation, microphones, press coverage.

Min. wage is $15/hr. for part time recruits, 4 hours guaranteed. I saw on Facebook Friday where a Muslim woman took the train on Wednesday from Brooklyn to DC (225 miles), spent the night, participated in the Hart Bldg. protest, and was back in Brooklyn Friday, exhilarated by her deed!

Found this on craigslist:

CRAIGSLIST: $35/HR FOR ANTI-TRUMP PROTESTERS IN PALOS VERDES TRUMP GOLF COURSE ,

DRESS TO IMPRESS, EXPECT TO STAY 10 HOURS – THAT'S $350 TOTAL... ANOTHER SOROS FUNDED RIOT TO COME?

Trump protesters needed $35 per hour – losangeles.craigslist.org losangeles.craigslist.org/wst/evg/5873600655.html...

(Palosverdes) hide this posting ... $35.00 per hour. QR Code Link to This Post. We are in need of protesters to help us stop Trump.

SIC 'EM DONALD!!!

Thought for the day July 2, 2018
Homemade signs

These are a few of the HATE signs at the protest Yesterday. They show great "creativity"! – Riiiight. Joke.

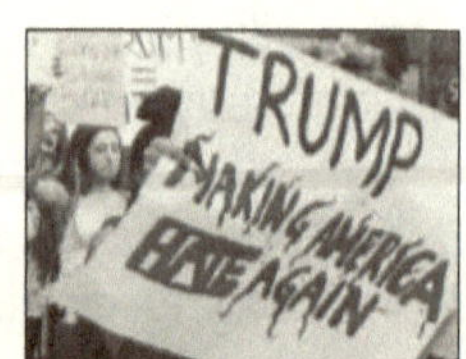

SIC 'EM DONALD!!!

Protest signs

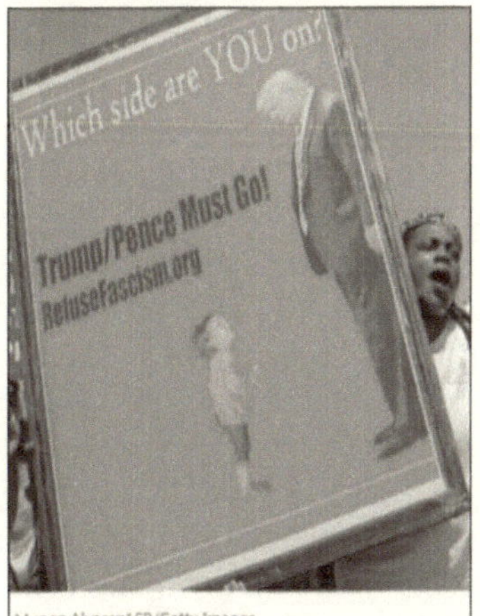

I sent you many 'protest' pictures yesterday of people getting paid to exercise their 1st Amendment right of 'free' speech, which cost Obama and Soros a BUNDLE to stage.

I suspect those pictures will get lost in the bowels of your computer, but this enlargement of Time Magazine's Fake Picture on a recent cover, modified, seems worthy of saving for the history books. Makes me realize (for sure), FAKE NEWS is the only weapon the Democrat Socialist Party has in their unrelenting effort to destroy America!!!!

And....I can't help but wonder "How much did this sign cost?"

SIC 'EM DONALD!!!

It is JULY 4, 2018
A good day to stop and say

" THANK YOU, LORD!"

Long may she wave

Stupidity

Stupidity is a lack of intelligence, understanding, reason, wit, or common sense.

(See Democratic party)

Thought for the day July 138, 2018
Incompetence

We are born ignorant. We, naturally, know how to scream and yell. With some effort, we learn to walk upright and feed ourselves.

As time goes by, some may acquire some knowledge, and/or intelligence. Some may acquire wisdom and common sense. Many acquire none of these traits. Result, incompetence and stupidity. Incompetence, camouflaged, by screaming and yelling,

Becomes transparent!!

SIC 'EM DONALD!!!

WALK AWAY MOVEMENT
Time will tell.

There is a movement among millennials called Walk Away.

What does it mean? Walk away from what?

The indication is They are leaving the Democrat Party.

Going where?

If they truly are adopting the Republican Party, it could be a blessing.

But if they are joining the Republican Party to push the Socialist agenda, that would be a curse.

Maybe they will be forming a 3rd party.

To do what?

THE SWAMP HAS MANY FACES.
SIC 'EM DONALD!!!

37 - TAXing

The IRS (almost) Criminal enterprise

The roots of IRS go back to the Civil War, when President Lincoln and Congress, in 1862, created the position of Commissioner of Internal Revenue and enacted an income tax to pay war expenses. The income tax was repealed 10 years later. But the idea would not go away. In 1894 the Supreme Court declared the Income Tax of 1894 unconstitutional in Pollock v. Farmers' Loan & Trust Co. In 1913 the 16th amendment was ratified, authorizing YOUR Federal government to tax your income, from any source. So, the idea of taxing your income was Resurrected in 1917 by the Progressive President Wilson, TO LAST FOREVER.

Today OUR IRS has 75,000 pages of rules, rules designed to make SURE you do not CHEAT our GUVMENT out of its 'Fair' share of 'OUR' money!!! And, to make SURE, 'OUR' IRS has about 93,000 employees, who are paid WELL with 'OUR' tax dollars. They range from Attorneys, return processors, officers who are armed to enforce the gillion tax laws, people who oversee operations, and clerks.

If you do not pay the correct amount of tax, according to THEIR rules, The IRS Gestapo can take money from your bank account, take your home and/or send you to jail. Sadly, even when you do everything right, a well-paid clerk, (who probably knows less about the 75,000 pages of rules than you do,) may misinterpret the law. Then you may get a letter from the IRS saying you did wrong. "Pay us 'OUR" money, or we will see you in court!!" It is now panic time. The IRS Budget, to make SURE you pay, and pay, and pay, is $13 billion plus. That is $140,000 per employee. How much do you make? THE FAIR TAX PLAN would eliminate most of this expense.

SIC 'EM DONALD!!!

Thought for the day July 8, 2018
"The Art of the Deal"

Successful negotiating is an art. All of us have been negotiating all of our lives, even as a child. Oh, we didn't call it by its name, and we have done it poorly. Mainly, we did it to get our way. We have done it by screaming, threatening, pouting, sometimes sweet talking, maybe with flowers. Maybe buying our way with money or making promises.

President Trump wrote a book entitled *The Art of the Deal*.

The World is now watching the Negotiation between USA and NOKO.

Being successful will follow these steps.
- Step 1. Establish a relationship.

Trump and Un did that in Singapore.
- Step 2. You catch more flies with Honey than salt.

Be honest. Insincerity is impossible to <u>camouflage</u>. Though difficult, Trump found something nice to say about Un. I think it was Theodore Roosevelt who said, "Speak softly but carry a big stick.'
- Step 3. Focus on WIN-WIN.

Successful negotiating ends in a WIN-WIN. Remember, WIN-LOSS is not a win at all.
- Step 4. Stay 'adult' at all times.

After the conclusion of Pompeo's meeting with NOKO, Pompeo remains upbeat, and positive. Signs of an adult. Unfortunately, NOKO has turned negative and childish.
- Step 5. Stay calm.

Don't push the relationship. Often silence and the passing of time is the strongest point. Have patience, but firm.
- Focus on WIN-WIN.

This is a complicated situation. It is obvious, a successful conclusion with take time and many meetings.

It is also obvious; the Media and Democrats will accentuate anything that appears negative.

DO NOT HAVE A FAINT HEART.
SIC 'EM DONALD!!!

REMEMBER THIS FROM JULY 8, 2016?
(Page 161 of my book My America is Back**)**

BJ Melton

Thought for today July 8, 2016

In times past, God has used many people for his purpose. Some I would not like, or agree with, But God did not consult me.

I'm not sure I would have liked Moses, but he was the right man for the time.

I know I would not have liked Pilate. He could have saved Christ from the cross, but it was God's plan that Christ be sacrificed for all of mankind.

So God provided Pilate.

Winston Churchill was one of our greatest national leaders in the 20th century. He was a bombastic, cigar smoking, at times crude, even misogynistic leader. A woman once told him he was disgustingly drunk.

His response was "My dear, you are disgustingly ugly, but tomorrow I shall be sober, and you will still be ugly!"

But he had exactly what was needed to stop Hitler at the Channel, to rouse a nation to never give up, and to partner with America to find final victory in Europe.

You wouldn't want him as your preacher, maybe not even your father, but he was the right leader for that moment in England's history.

Do we have a Jesus running for President?

Of course not, but we do have a devil like person running,

A candidate we know will continue taking America into the abyss. So we must consider someone else who is imperfect, someone who will shape the culture in America for the next 30 years.

So, then, where will Donald Trump take us? I ask myself will Donald be good for America? I honestly believe that he has been already.

He has shaken the political system to its greedy roots! Do his comments offend me? At times. Do I agree with all he says? Not at all. Is he being raised up by God to preserve America? Time will tell. This I know. Donald is the only choice for Americas' survival.

SO... SIC 'EM DONALD!

Subject: Special news bulletin
JULY 9, 2018 10 PM

NEWS FLASH: TRUMP NOMINATES BRETT KAVANAUGH FOR SUPREME

COURT JUSTICE. AMERICANS APPLAUDED.

NEWS FLASH: PROTESTERS ORGINIZED AND PAID FOR, BY OBAMA, SOROS AND LIBERAL DEMOCRATS, TAKE TO THE STREETS WITH THEIR BOUGHT AND PAID FOR PROFESSIONALLY MADE SIGNS. THEY HAD SIGNS IN WAITING FOR ANYONE WHO MIGHT HAVE BEEN NOMINATED.

THEY WERE IN THE STREETS, WITH MICROPHONES, LOUD SPEAKERS, SCREAMING THEIR

PROFESSIONALLY WRITTEN WORDS, WHICH MADE NO SENSE. MEANWHILE, OBAMA, MICHELLE, AND VALERIE GARRETT, SAT IN THEIR #10,000/MONTH RENT HOUSE, AND SMILED AND SMIRKED AT THEIR HANDIWORK.

SIC 'EM DONALD!!!

Thought for the day July 10, 2018
Follow me on this.

Paul Ryan is Speaker of the House of Representatives.

His salary is $223,500/yr.

Paul Ryan is a Rino. Rinos are disguised Democrats.

Ryan will retire in January 2019 at age 48.

THAT'S FORTY-EIGHT YEARS OLD! On a pension of at least $223,500. How is that for "Social Security" and he never paid a dime in to it!

(I paid into 'my' Social Security for 50 years.

People like Ryan Stole all of it.

Now, I am supposed to be beholding to them for my Social Security 'benefit'. But that's another story.) Someone will replace Ryan. WHO?

Currently, Jim Jordan, a strong conservative, is favored.

By Republicans, NOT Democrats.

He will push the Trump agenda.

Uh Oh. Out of the blue come some charges of sexual abuse, NOT by Jordan, but for Jordan NOT reporting something he supposedly knew about.

It was 28 years ago. 28 years? <u>Why now?</u>

Destroy Jordan!!!

How convenient! The assumed guilty person is not around to be interrogated. He died in 2005.

The democrats know if elected Speaker, he will mess in their mess kit.

He must be destroyed!

Remember 30-year-old events dug up and ballyhooed about Trump?

Same reason -destroy Trump!!

It is a game called "Destroy" and Democrats play it over and over.

The obvious becomes obvious!!!!

If it is good for America, it is terrible for Democrats!

SIC 'EM JIM!!!

July 10, 2018

Added thought by Jim DeMint

Jim Jordan Is A Man of Integrity Being Railroaded With Fact less Allegations

When I read the actual stories under those headlines, my reaction turned from dread to outrage. Jim Jordan isn't being accused; he's being railroaded.

By Jim DeMint
JULY 10, 2018
Like many Americans, when I saw last week's headlines about my friend,

U.S. Rep. Jim Jordan (R-Ohio), I couldn't believe them. The accusations did not describe the man of character and courage I've known for more than a decade. When I read the actual stories under those headlines, my reaction turned from dread to outrage. Jordan isn't being accused; <u>he's being</u>

<u>railroaded.</u> Some of the former wrestlers, including two with criminal pasts, are now accusing Jordan of knowingly turning a blind eye to Strauss's

alleged abusive behavior. Other former OSU wrestlers spoke with

the Washington Post, including Michael Alf, who said Jordan was, "the most honest person I've ever met. The thing is, if he saw something like that, he wouldn't have tolerated it. People like Jim spend a lifetime developing a reputation of honesty and integrity, yet irresponsible media try to destroy that reputation with one misleading story.

Thought for the day July 11, 2018
A WOMAN'S RIGHT?

When Justice Kennedy announced his retirement as a Supreme Court Justice on June 27, the Antifa, Obama-led protesters began their plan to protest Whoever President Trump might nominate. Protest leaders were lined up, protesters recruited and paid, professional signs printed, arrangements for liberal press coverage were made, speakers with microphones, and foghorns were arranged for.

Monday night at 9:05 all Mouths were opened, and the screaming began as expected.

Vulgar signs, profanity, gross idiot type behavior went rampant.

"Save Planned Parenthood" " Save Roe vs Wade" "Protect a woman's right".

I find <u>woman's right</u> to kill her 'unborn' child disturbing.

Think about this:

After an ecstatic moment in woman's life, God placed a person in her womb. She <u>voluntarily</u> <u>adopted</u> this new person, an she obligated herself to carry it in her womb, nourish it as it grows for about 9 months, then present this GOD GIVEN person to world, give it a name, and continue nourishing it until it can become independent and care for itself. Never, in the scheme of things, does a woman have the 'right' to slay another person.

This person she carries in her womb has as much RIGHT to life as the person carrying it. Killing this person is NOT a right, it is murder!

Since Roe vs Wade was passed, over 60,000,000

DEFENSELESS PERSONS have been killed and buried in the trash dump. And we are a 'civilized' nation?

38 – Electoral College

Thought for the day July 13, 2018

 **On the lighter side**
This being Friday the 13th, it might be bad luck to get too serious about anything or anybody.

There was a circus in town yesterday. There were elephants snorting, jackasses braying, and clowns cavorting, all trying to get in Ring one at the same time.

Unorganized chaos. Our Congress on public display.

Peter Strzok appeared before a Congressional Committee yesterday. He was there to answer questions about his promise and guarantee to stop Trump from being elected President.

It was a funny day. Republicans asked pointed questions about the subject. Democrats talked about everything BUT the subject. Most questions he did not answer.

A few he did answer, but with double talk. When something 'touchy' showed up, Democrats would interrupt, talk, shout, and generally be despicably rude. Anything to bog down the proceeding and keep anything from being accomplished.

In short, they exposed their 'real' classy self, for all America to see. It was wonderful. I had to laugh, watching them show everybody what a bunch of unfunny clowns they are. I had a real belly laugh when Strzok said he was "NOT BIASED". The bias list is long. One of his best statements was when he said, "Hillary will beat Trump 100,000,000 votes to Zero".

No bias there!

You don't want to know how much it cost 'us' to learn nothing yesterday, except we have more jackasses in Congress than we realized.

The swamp runs deep!

SIC 'EM DONALD!!!

Thought for the day July 14, 2018
Electoral College

Today has been a wonderful day. I have watched many video clips of several dozen 'famous' people guaranteeing Trump

1. Would not be a candidate for President.
2. If he ran, he would never be nominated
3. If, by remote chance he is nominated, Clinton would bury him!

In retrospect, watching these 'intelligent' people proclaim their prognostications so positively, and in such a condescending way, it provided me with many laughs today.

Even on election night this map predicted the final result.

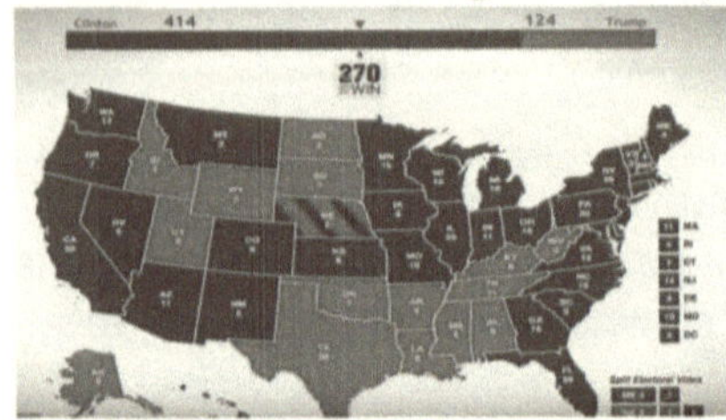
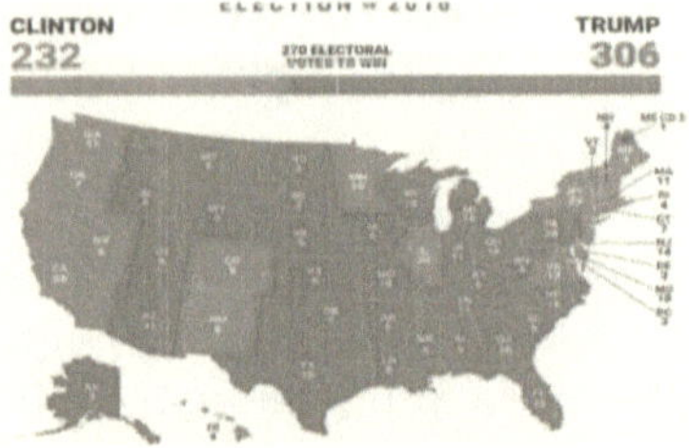

November 8   November 9

Map shows Trump winning 15 states.   He won 32 states.
Question 1: How could so many 'intellectuals' be wrong?
Trump is our President. Millions of Americans know that.
Question 2: How can so many think Hillary or Obama is President?
It is my opinion, (a right I still have, but is weakening), the "gimme, gimme" attitude that has encompassed America, has destroyed the values America was founded on.

SIC 'EM DONALD!!! MAGA!!!

THOUGHT FOR THE DAY JULY 16, 2018

President Trump in London

There is no limit.

Obama and Soros will spend any amount of money to 'try' to embarrass President Trump, to degrade his accomplishments, and to create hate for him.

When he visited England this weekend, they hired protestors, made signs, and, get this, they visualized this giant baby balloon of Trump flying over London.

However, it flopped. never got more than 30 feet off the ground.
Cost a lot of money, but what is money to Obama & Soros!
SIC 'EM DONALD!!

Thought for the day July 17, 2018

It seems like, everybody thinks Putin wanted Trump to win.

Except me.

Common sense tells me different.

Follow me on this.

The <u>Crimean peninsula</u> was <u>annexed</u> from <u>Ukraine</u> by the <u>Russian Federation</u> in February–March 2014.

Putin showed signs recreating the original USSR.

OBAMA DID NOTHING.

Obama whispered a message for Putin before his reelection in 2012

"Tell Putin after the election I'll have more flexibility" (on a hot mike) Hillary helped Russia set up 'Silicon Valley' just outside of Moscow, and $millions went into the Clinton foundation.

Hillary approved selling 20% of our uranium reserves to Russia.

What a friend, and more millions to the Foundation.

Slick Willie gave a speech in Moscow. Was paid $500,000. How can you reconcile Putin wanting Trump to win, when he had patsies, Hillary and Obama, in his pocket?

The famous DOSSIER, originated in Russia, and paid for by the DNC, was calculated to guarantee Hillary's election.

PUTIN WANTED TRUMP TO WIN? STUPID.

Despite what you may 'think' you saw and what you <u>will</u> hear from

Trump haters about his meeting with Putin——— THE PROOF WILL BE IN THE EATING AND THE TABLE IS JUST NOW BEING SET!!

Remember 'Rocket man' from North Korea?

Many may be eating crow, not cake.

SIC 'EM DONALD!!!

Thought for the day July 18, 2018
Imagination!

"♫Imagination is funny

It makes a cloudy day sunny

Makes a bee think of honey♫"

The last few days with Trump and Putin have stirred my imagination.

Imagination IS funny, crazy, silly. It can create joy, happiness, or sadness and despair, or great inventions. When I was a boy, in my mind, Tarzan, Mickey Mouse, Tom Sawyer, The Shadow, Alley Oop and his dinosaur, Dinny, Alice in Wonderland, and Rip Van Winkle, were all real. I swung through the trees on grapevine, road Tarzan's elephant, solved many crimes with the Shadow, rode a barge on the Mississippi River.

With imagination, anything was possible.

Walt Disney used 'imagination' to make $billions$.

Back to Trump and Putin.

Imagine you are hidden in the room where they met alone, except for interpreters. What did they talk about? Were they courteous, loud, rude, telling jokes, having a leisure dinner, cursing each other? Were there threats of war, or sanctions.

Did they agree on anything? If so, what?

We can imagine, BUT we do not know.

THEN, they stood before the world and answered questions.

Afterward, they smiled and shook hands.

Are they 'friends' now or still enemies? Will they meet again?

Was there something good Accomplished?

Many thought the meeting was good thing.

Then there are the naysayers.

"He committed treason!"

"He gave away the store."

"Putin made a fool of him!"

"He missed his chance to call Putin the Tyrant, that he his." "Russia is our enemy, not our friend!"

HATE for Trump is on the front burner.

THE NAYSAYERS DON'T KNOW WHAT HAPPENED.

As I have said "The proof is in the eating. The table has just been set." Many will eat crow. Imagination can be evil.

SIC 'EM DONALD!!!

Thought for the day July 19, 2018

The 'Movement'

New York congressional candidate Alexandria Ocasio-Cortez has called on protesters rallying under the "Abolish ICE" banner to occupy border crossings, airports and Immigration and Customs Enforcement (ICE) offices across the country.

THIS WOMAN IS A FULL-BLOOD SOCIALIST COMMUNIST. BERNIE SANDERS, COMPARED TO HER, WOULD BE A CHRISTIAN CAPITALIST.

And she is 'smart', too. Check out this statement. "The reason unemployment is so low, everybody has two jobs".

????????????????

Read it slowly again....................

If elected in November, she will contest Maxine Waters for "Running off at the mouth" champion, and along with Nancy Pelosi, form a trio for the "I can't believe she said that!" club.

Who is she, really?

Well, she graduated from Boston College, got a job as a bartender, then as an aide to Sen. Ted Kennedy, where Moveon.org (Soros) found her and is now making her rich.

Will she be elected in Socialist New York?

Almost certainly!!!!!

SIC 'EM DONALD!!

Thought for the day July 24, 2018

More hate

I sit here at this computer, day after day, reading and writing e-mail, watching the stock market, reading fake and real news, and THINKING. For several days, I have been thinking about Helsinki, and the historic meeting between Trump and Putin. I read what some Democrats say about Trump and the "failed" meeting, and I think DEMOCRATS!!

I have heard about Democrats since I was a boy. In the last 80 years, I have experienced

FDR, HST, JFK, LBJ, Jimmy Carter, Bill Clinton, and Barrack HUSSEIN Obama.

FDR started the Welfare State game, LBJ sold tickets,

Clinton collected the money, and Obama put millions in the stadium.

Democrats have evolved from a "Good ole boy' party into a Socialist-Communist organization that actually HATES America.

President Trump was chastised, and even accused of Treason.

All because he wants to MAKE AMERICA GREAT AGAIN.

If it is good for America, Democrats hate it. The uninformed and unwashed march in the streets with their professionally made signs, preaching HATE for YOU, our President, and degrading America.

Then, they back up to Obama's cash register to get their protest pay!

Democrats are not Democrats anymore.

This old world is changing.

The table has now been set for something great to happen.

North Korea, Russia, and, as of YESTERDAY, Iran, are seated.

What will happen? We don't know.

As I have said the proof is in the eating, so, put on your bib!

SIC 'EM DONALD!!!

Thought for the day July 26, 2018
Looking a life in a rear-view mirror

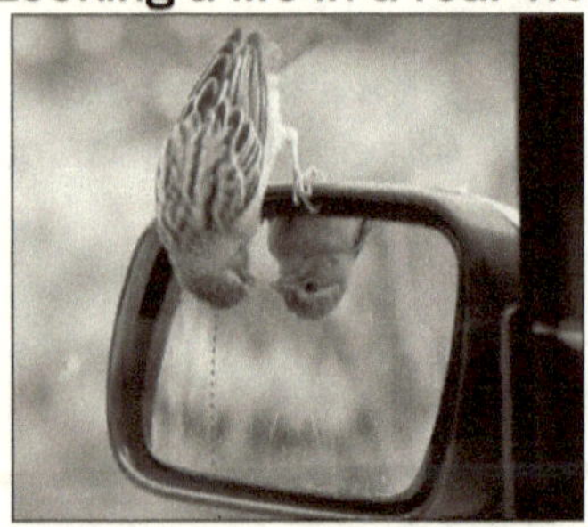

How many crises have you experienced in your life?

How many were catastrophic? At the time, did the world end? I know, in my life, there have been many unpleasant events, a few of which made me ask "Why me Lord?"

Some were actually life changing, but most were just disappointments. The death of my daughter, the death of my son, the unexpected death of my Papa, the untimely death of my first wife after 46 years, learning I had prostate cancer, were life changing.

Very sad events. Many tears were shed, many questions asked. Then, in retrospect, there were broken hearts, lost sweethearts, disappointment in several jobs I did not get, promotions that passed me by, 'friends' that betrayed me, games that we lost, crucial putts I did not make.

No crisis is trivial at the moment, and life is not always fair.

Sic 'Em Donald!

But each event was a learning experience for me, a fork in the road.
Like I said, many were life changing.

Looking in the rear-view mirror, most, but not all, so called crises happened for the best.

With all this experience I have learned much. I should be perfect, but my Sweetheart wife reminds me daily that I am not even close. So, life moves on.

I can't change the past. It is what it is, and I don't know the future. This I do know:

IF I SPEND MY TIME LOOKING IN THE REAR VIEW MIRROR, THE FUTURE WILL BE A WRECK!

Think about it.

SIC 'EM DONALD!!!

39 – Not Funny Funny

Thought for the day July 27, 2018

Not funny Funny

Sometimes funny things happen. You know, we call them funny, but they are probably not funny, just funny.

A funny thing happened to me this week.

Tuesday, the 24th, was Clarene's birthday. I got on the internet and ordered her favorite smell good stuff. It was to come from NEW YORK, and since I was late ordering, I asked for 2nd day delivery.

OK. Done deal.

Also, on Tuesday, I ordered a Beauty Rest king size mattress. Our current mattress is a 20-year-old Sleep Number. Mattress people say we should replace a mattress after 10 years of service, so we got to thinking about a new one.

I found the one we think we want on the internet and called them.

Guess what? You won't believe this but the man who answered, had a strong!!! accent, and was hard to understand, plus the fidelity of his phone was bad.

I managed to place my order. He said it would arrive in 7-10 days. I complained.

Did I tell you he is in New York, also?

In a little bit, he said "I found one in a warehouse in Texas, we can ship it immediately. Should arrive by Thursday." Bear in mind, all this is what I 'think' he said.

OK. Done deal.

Wednesday morning, I started getting tracking e-mails from USPS telling me my item would be delivered by 8:00 PM Thursday.

I thought it a little strange shipping a mattress by USPS, so I checked my paperwork, and sure enough, it said they ship by FedEx, UPS, and USPS.

So, Thursday we stripped our mattress to the bare, and waited.

About 7 PM, no mattress, so I called Beauty Rest. Same man answered.

"My mattress is not here!" He said, "Takes 7-10 days." "You told me Thursday!!!" "Takes 7-10 days" Hang up.

Then I discovered an e-mail from USPS which said Item delivered to mailbox at 1:30 PM. So, I went out to the mailbox to get my mattress.

I found a box with Clarene's cologne. Made Clarene happy.

FUNNY THINGS HAPPEN. MADE MY FACE RED

Thought for the day July 28, 2018
CHOICES

Have you ever thought about the choices you make?

You make them every day and have since you were born.

Even a baby may choose its mother' milk or reject it.

In every situation, you have a choice.

As a child you were told by your parents to do something.

You have a decision to make.

Do I do it? Do I not do it?

Either way there are consequences.

As a parent you choose how to raise your children.

Do you discipline them? Do you let run the store?

Either way there are consequences.

Did you choose to be a leader, or follower? Maybe you chose to be a joiner.

Either way there are consequences.

Did you choose to be responsible or irresponsible?

There are joiners and followers marching in the streets today, not knowing why, and totally irresponsible for their actions.

The streets of San Francisco, and other cities, are crawling with "homeless' people. Somewhere along the way, consciously or unconsciously, they made choices that has led them to a cardboard shelter begging for food and drugs and defecating in the street.

As a boy I chose to be responsible for me. It never occurred me that government or RICH people owed me anything. I worked and I got paid for being productive. It was my money, but, by force, government took part of it. As time went by, I forked over more and more.

You see, gradually, liberal thinking people convinced millions to be irresponsible.

"Let us take care of you. WE will be Responsible for you. You have a RIGHT to free schooling, free health care, part of the rich people's money, a 'good' job (if you want it). WE are compassionate and caring. Come lay your sweet head on my bosom. Worry about nothing. WE will tax the rich."

Result: A Welfare State of people who are totally irresponsible.

A welfare state that breeds the likes of Nancy Pelosi, Chuck Schumer, Bernie Sanders, and Maxine Waters, all millionaires who (they say) want to punish other millionaires. (but not themselves)

President Trump got taxes cut and his actions have created millions of jobs.

SIC 'EM DONALD!!!

Thought for the day July 29, 2018
More Hate

Today Is Sunday, the first day of a new week.

Of the 7 days in a week, 6 are just plain vanilla, But Sunday is special. Today I got up thinking about Jesus and what he did for me. I think about him preaching 'love thy neighbor', 'do unto others....'. I will go to church this morning and in my feeble way, try to honor Jesus with songs and prayer and thanksgiving. At the same time, I can't help but think how the world was in Jesus' time. It was evil to the core. Morality was 'anything goes', 'if it feels good, do it'.

Sound familiar?

Jesus came with a mission, preaching about the Kingdom of God.

A new king? Whoa. This won't do.

When King Herod heard that a "king" was born,

he ordered all boys under 2 years to be slain. There was weeping and gnashing of teeth, but Jesus escaped to Egypt. At about 30 years of age, Jesus started preaching salvation, and changing the world. Soon thousands were following him and praising him. But the democrats and socialists of the day (Scribes and Pharisees) were having none of it, and started planning to kill him, and they did! Today, we have a simile of a sort.

President Trump is not a Jesus, but he is a man with a mission, determined to change America for the better. Millions are following him!

Whoa! That won't do!

The Democrats and Socialist, who, two years ago,

preached "LOVE NOT HATE", don't want to change, and have set about to destroy President Trump. Now there is no Love, just HATE for Trump. This past week, Maxine Waters stood in the pulpit of a 'church', claiming she was instructed by GOD to destroy Trump and she was on her way to Washington, DC to do just that!!

Sorry, Maxine, my GOD would not tell you that. My GOD is loving, kind and wants only good for everyone. Apparently, the DEVIL has been talking to you and you have gotten in bed with him, hoping to get a reserved seat in Hell. And, frankly, I think you have earned it.

SIC 'EM DONALD!!!

Thought for the day July 30, 2018
FREE STUFF

"You have a right"!!!!! Screams the liberal politician. I saw red faced Bernie Sanders screaming at the top of his voice about my 'rights'. I have a 'right' to:

Free health care

A job with a living wage

A nice place to live

Free college tuition

A nice car, TV, cell phone

I am so naive. You see, I have lived nearly 93 years and, until now, didn't know I had a 'right' to all this FREE Stuff. Now I am angry. The only thing I ever got free was poison ivy. Everything else I have paid for with wages I received by working and making money for my wage payer.

I know it is against 'Liberal' rules to think, but I am a dyed-the -wool conservative and I have a 'right' to think, so here goes.

FREE health care. (liberal noise)

I get sick and go to a nice hospital. The hospital cost a lot of money to build. I get_free room and board._ They have the latest diagnostic equipment, which cost money. It is used to diagnose my problem. No cost to me. My nurse is working a 12-hour shift to make money for her family. She spent years of her life training to give me_free care.

My doctor lived like a pauper for 8-10 years learning to be the best doctor he can be, now cares for me at no cost.

Being conservative I know all this care cost money. Where does it come from? TAX THE RICH!!! Of course. No problem. It is only right that the RICH, who have been so 'lucky' to have money, should share their wealth to pay for my 'rights'. Finally, it seems, the RICH pay for all the 'rights' of liberals, and that privilege IS THE ONLY RIGHT the RICH have.

It is called 'income re-distribution' which leads to Utopia.

Liberals know this theory will get lots of votes.

If you rob Peter to pay Paul, millions will claim to be Paul.

Think about it. There really is NO FREE LUNCH!

SIC 'EM DONALD!!!

Thought for the day July 31, 2018

FREE STUFF # 2

Bernie Sanders keeps screaming Free Tuition for everybody.

I wonder how is this possible, so I did some checking.

At Yale, tuition, room and board, books and misc. is $65,000/semester.

For a full year that is $130,000, and for 4 years, a HALF A MILLION!

For 1000 students, you are now talking real money- $500,000,000!!!!! Professors are paid (I didn't say earned) on average $195,000, and associate professors around $100,000. (You wonder why they don't teach for FREE as they fill our young people's heads with mush about the joys of socialism and all this free stuff they are 'entitled to)

For 200 professors and associates, add another $30,000,000/year, or $120,000,000 for 4 years.

If you assume a million students nationwide, which, if it is FREE, is not unrealistic.

So, what have we got? $500,000 times 1 million students plus $ 120,000,000 million times 100 universities, is what for 4 years? Boggles my mind.

My math says $620 billion or over a half a trillion!!!!!!!!!!!!!!!!!!!

The old saying 'Liars figure, and figures lie' is true here, because

I do not know what the real cost would be,

I JUST KNOW WE ARE TALKING ABOUT A <u>WHOLE LOT OF MONEY!!!</u>

Where would all this money come from?

That is a silly question.

We tax the rich, of course.

SIC 'EM DONALD!!!

Thought for the day Aug 1, 2018

FREE STUFF # 3

Bernie Sanders believes everybody who wants to work, should have a job that pays a 'living wage', whatever that is.

Sunday after church my wife and I had lunch at Brahms.

There in the window beside us was a sign"

HIRING

Store managers

Assistant store managers

Shift supervisors

Sic 'Em Donald!

    Sales persons

    Chefs

Once a week we have crispy tacos from Taco Bell.

They have similar sign of Help Wanted.

Last week when I left with my order, there in the median just across the street, stood a healthy-looking man with a cardboard sign which read "Help. Will work for food".

I stopped long enough to tell him "Taco Bell is hiring"

On Tuesday, Church's Chicken has a leg and thigh for $1.49. I ate there yesterday. While eating, I was approached by a nice looking, well-dressed black lady, probably in her 30's. She asked me for $3.50 for bus fare to where she lives in 'far' North Dallas. When I asked her questions, she asked if she could sit down, and I said OK. I asked her if she had a job and she said no. I said there are lots of jobs available. Why don't you get a job? She said she was on 'disability', and kinda rolled her shoulder a little. If she got a job, she would lose her disability pay!!!! When it became apparent I didn't have $3.50, she asked if I would buy her something to eat. I said you can eat what I am eating, and I gave her $2.00 change I had from paying for mine.

She took the $2.00 and walked out the door, never to be seen again.

So, what can I learn from all of this? When I look at these 2 cases, and see pictures of "homeless" crawling in the street, the only logical conclusion I can come to is:

SOME PEOPLE DO NOT WANT TO WORK!!

Some, I am sure, are college graduates whose self-worth has been so magnified by their left-wing professors, they are unwilling to accept a demeaning job on the first step of the ladder. "If I can't start at the Top, forget it!"

Like Jesus said: "The poor you have with you always". Now you know why.

SIC 'EM DONALD!!!

40 – Man of the Year

Thought for the day Aug. 2, 2018
TIME MAGAZINE-TREASON IN YOUR FACE!!

MAN OF THE YEAR!

A little history to think about!
(2 years ago today. Page 173 of "My America is Back")

Thought for the day Aug. 3, 2016
Well, I had one Happy day-Monday.

Obama ruined yesterday and I have carry over today.

Obama had the gall, and audacity, to say Trump "is not fit to be President."

Sic 'Em Donald!

This from a man who soaked up 'REV.' Jeremiah Wright's hate for America for 20 years, a man who sat at the feet of <u>Bill Ayers, who had been a domestic terrorist</u> who planted bombs in public places, including the Pentagon. A man who is a self-confessed Muslim who bowed to the King of Saudi Arabia, a man who has filled the White House with Muslims and Muslim sympathizers, a man who has dedicated himself to reducing America to 3rd world status. A man who is flooding America with Muslim immigrants, some of which are terrorists.

Obama was elected, not because he was qualified, but<u> solely</u> because he is half black. He was not fit to be President when he was elected, and he has severely deteriorated with ON-THE-JOB-TRAINING.

So I repeat: <u>Obama had the gall, and audacity, to say Trump "is not fit to be President."</u> <u>Lies are a way of life for socialist, communists and Muslims.</u>

SIC 'EM DONALD!!!

Thought for the day Aug. 3, 2018

I didn't know this. Did you?

For years I have seen gold advertised as a hedge against inflation.

Buy it now. Gold is going to $2000/oz.

Sounds wonderful. Maybe I SHOULD buy some.

But I procrastinate. Fortunately!

This week I saw an ad for Liberty gold coins.

Good name, Right?

Price was $129.95 for a gold dollar.

So, I googled it. Bear in mind, gold on the market Friday was $1213 per ounce.

I asked google how much the gold in a Liberty gold dollar was worth. Answer: $59.00. Then I learn about 'carat'.

I learn about 10 carat, 12 carat, 16 carat, etc.

24 carat is 99.95% gold and you can buy a

24 carat gold coin for about $1325, $100 over market value. Might be a good deal if you think you can wait for gold to reach $2000.

Personally, I am pretty sure I can't wait.

Selling gold seems like a scam to me.

PS: I saw where you can buy a 99.9% silver dollar for $135, plus S&H. Market value for silver about $15/oz. AREN'T YOU GLAD YOU

BJ Melton

KNOW ALL OF THIS!!! MADE YOUR DAY!

Count your blessings.

How many times have you heard that? A million, maybe?

In my case, the blessing list is long, and I am thankful. But some blessings are fickle. Some we don't even think about.

until they are gone.

Take teeth, for example. We just chew and brush, day after day.

A real blessing.

Unfortunately, for some, one day they are gone, and are replaced by fake ones. When I was young, I could hear a pin drop on a rug next door.

A real blessing.

Today, it is HUH? What did you say? Talk a little louder, please. I have played a lot of golf. For many years I see that little ball, no matter where it went, and I went walking to hit it again.

A real blessing.

Today I have cataracts, and wear glasses, and still lose sight of the ball, even though when I hit it, it ends up a lot closer to me than it once did.

Understand?

As a boy I remember running everywhere I went. Never got tired. In college, playing football, I was given the name LEGS Melton. I had good, real strong legs. A real blessing.

Today I have a knee I was not born with, have had two back operations, running is only a memory, and walking has become work, one careful step at a time.

In summary, I still have most of my teeth, no problem.

Not hearing good can be a REAL blessing.

With my 'aids' I see pretty good.

But my legs —— there is no fix for my legs.

I know there are canes, and walkers, and other gadgets to make me somewhat mobile, but they are just patches for a real problem-limited use of my legs.

However, I am still blessed because I HAVE TWO LEGS, SOMEWHAT USABLE!

And that is an AMEN!

PS: I have golf clubs for sale, some really good, some seen better days. 40-year-old PIOT PUTTER not for sale.

BJM

Thought for the day Aug. 6, 2018
Candace Owens

News flash: "To be clear: ANTIFA, <u>an all-white fascist organization,</u> just grew violent and attacked an all-black and Hispanic police force.

Because I, a BLACK woman, was eating breakfast.

Is this the civil rights era all over again?"

The story. Candace is a black, conservative woman.

She was eating breakfast in a Philadelphia hotel with a friend, when ANTIFA protesters saw her and barged in to where she was eating.

They were removed but waited outside for her and her friend to exit.

They were cursed, harassed, and spit on.

Black and Hispanic police, protecting them, were attacked.

So, this is the "Democratic" party today?

Hitler was the #1 fascist of the 20th century.

I wonder who is sponsoring ANTIFA? Is it SOROS and Obama?

SIC 'EM DONALD!!!

Thought for the day Aug.8, 2018
MY WORLD

You know, I can't understand the world some people live in.

We have socialist and conservative TV stations who preach their stuff, day in and day out.

Some of us search for threads of truth in the fake news. Some step on facts and search for more garbage. For over 2 years, even the slightly informed people know Hillary Clinton and the Democratic Party hired a man to create a cock-and-bull story (dossier) aimed at discrediting Donald Trump, so Hillary would win the election.

NOW HEAR THIS.

Today I listened to a reporter interviewing a number of Trump protesters. Her approach to each was: "Do you think it was right for TRUMP to hire a foreigner to dig up dirt on Hillary Clinton?" A non-fact to start with, but none corrected her. They all parroted the same story.

"NO! He is a liar." A little old lady, holding an "Impeach Trump" sign "Mueller will get him, will impeach him. He is a disgrace." One woman, (a librarian she said,) was wearing a statue of liberty crown said " Since I am librarian, I have to know the facts, and Trump stole the election. Impeach him!"

Not only are these people ignorant, they apparently don't work, unless you call walking the street, carrying vulgar signs, and screaming obscenities, work. Wonder where they get money? Welfare? Disability? Soros? Obama?

They all looked well fed.

They are not in my world!

SIC 'EM DONALD!!!

Thought for the day Aug.9, 2018

ANTIFA

In 2017 at a Trump rally in Berkeley, Ca., a professor who teaches Ethics at a local college, participated in an ANTIFA protest group.

He wore black, was hooded, and had a mask.

He carried a bike chain with lock attached, with which he assaulted 7 trump supporters, beating them on the head causing severe injury.

He was charged with 4 felony counts for assault, with a deadly weapon. His trial was this week. He has spent no jail time.

His sentence: 3-month probation.

Question: If you should do what he did, what would be your sentence?

Think about it.

These ANTIFA groups are fascist pigs, Obama's secret army.

SIC 'EM DONALD!!!

41 – SCAM

Scam-Thought for the day Aug. 14, 2018

SCAM NOTICE

I have done business for many years with a CVS store 1/2 mile from my house.

Yesterday an authentic looking email appeared in my email box from CVS. It was a survey wanting my opinion of CVS.

Since I have SPENT thousands with them over the years, it seemed to be a reasonable request.

The survey was simple, even a child could do it. After answer all the questions in the affirmative, CVS was so grateful, they offered me a free gift of my choice.

Just pay shipping and handling!!!!!!!!!!!!!

(I been here before, but I didn't see it coming-SCAM) So, they need my credit card.

I picked a beautiful watch (which I do not need, (IT WAS FREE!!) Last night Discover sent me a Fraud warning.

"Call this number immediately"

Thought for the day Aug. 15, 2018

Headline July 1, 1970

WE WILL RUN OUT OF OIL BY 2015!

Every 10-15 years, it seems like those with money create
a scheme to make more money.
Such was the artificially created hoax of the 1970's.
The story goes that there was no more oil to be discovered.
Gasoline was rationed. Long lines, 50-100 cars long, were common place.
Ten gallon purchase was maximum. Price per gallon $4.50+
Many times, waiting in line for hours, when you got to the pump
there was a sign "SOLD OUT".
By 1975, things had returned to 'normal.'
Some made money. Peasants lost money.
The hoax died.
Now it is 2018,
and we are shipping energy to any country willing to pay for it.
Unless you were born before 1960, You did not experience this hoax.
There are more to come.
Stay tuned.

On checking, sure enough, it IS fraud. Unknowingly, in small print somewhere, I agreed to pay a monthly fee (for nothing).

I think it has now been cancelled.

Sadly, I knew better. There is NO FREE LUNCH!

In retrospect, CVS doesn't need my opinion on anything.

In futurespect, if it's free, it really ain't! Not all the crooks are in Washington.

Thought for the day Aug. 16, 2018
Social Security, the perpetual hoax.

Roosevelt, a democrat, signed SS into law Aug. 15, 1935.

I, We, You, could "voluntarily' have up to 1% taken from our earnings, UP TO $1400!

This money was to be placed in a separate SS Trust Fund and saved for my retirement. Everybody had a unique SS number. While I was working, I could call SS and find out how much money was in "my" account.

Today, if you are working, 6.2% is withheld on what you earn up to about $125,000.

Today, millions of retirees receive a monthly check from the "Fund".

Today, millions of legal and illegal immigrants,

(who paid nothing into the "Fund"), receive payments from the "Fund." Today, at least 40% of recipients have no other source of income. Today, if your income, including SS, is over $24,000, you pay income tax on up to 85% of your SS payments. Today, and for decades, Democrats have run on the platform "Better vote for me. Republicans been gonna take away your SS", literally scaring millions of the uninformed into voting democrat!!!

FOR YOUR INFORMATION!!!

President Johnson, a democrat, transferred the "Untouchable" Trust Fund to the General fund in 1965 and spent much of it.

Wiped it out!!! Now we are dependent on money for SS payments being included in the General Fund.

Plus, since 1965, both democrat and Republican Presidents have used SS money to help reduce spending deficits.

Bunch of crooks!

The perpetual HOAX!

TAX REFORM. SIC 'EM DONALD!!!

Thought for the day Aug. 17, 2018

The Hole in the ozone HOAX.

Follow me on this.

In 1977, Pawan Bhartia had finished his PHD in Physics with no job in sight.

He answered a <u>CONTRACTOR FOR NASA ad</u> for "Atmospheric Scientist".

Having no knowledge of what the job was about, he got the job.

His job was to study Ozone- What it is, Where is it, What it does, and how is it beneficial to humans?

Let's start with this: <u>Ozone</u> -- O_3 –comprises 0.000007% of the atmosphere, or about

0.3 of a molecule per million!

Right here, I have to put the cart before the horse.

They concluded there is a giant hole in the Ozone layer over the Antarctica!

This was worldwide frantic news. What caused it? BEFORE I lose you, Hear this! They (whoever 'they' is) claim Ozone protects you from ultra-violet rays from the sun. IF MANKIND DOES ANYTHING TO DESTROY OZONE, UV RAYS WOULD CAUSE GROSS SKIN CANCER AND DEATHS! So, with that in mind, Pawan and others set out to learn about Ozone. First, they made "assumptions" about ozone. Second, they made plans to prove their assumptions. They gathered data from Weather balloons, and special instrumentation from space craft circling the earth.

They accumulated millions and millions of bits of information.

In analyzing and interpreting this 'data', most of it did not agree with their 'assumptions' and was discarded.

They concluded:

1. The "thickness" of the ozone 'layer' varies at points around the globe.

2.The thickness changes during the day.

The hole over Antarctica was caused by CFCS (refrigerants).

The hole started forming in 1970. 5. Reason: -CFCS escaped in to the atmosphere, combined with Ozone to create something useless and destroying Ozone molecules. (AT THIS POINT YOU NEED TO KNOW CFCS IS

HEAVIER THAN AIR AND WOULD STAY ON THE GROUND-NOT ASCEND!!!!!)

Now I have a question: If they did not know about the 'supposed' HOLE until 1985, who can say (IF there is one) the hole was not there in 1960 Or 1860? AND Why, Why, Why, did the 'hole' form over

Antarctica, on the bottom of the earth, when most use of CFCs is In the Northern hemisphere?

The effect of the HOAX. THE BILLION DOLLAR REFRIGERATION BUSINESS

WAS TURNED UPSIDE DOWN FINDING 'NON-HARMFUL REFRIGERANTS', AND REDESIGN OF

EQUIPMENT.

The <u>whole hole hoax</u> cost millions of dollars, and made millionaires of a few.

Next: Global warming Hoax

Thought for the day Aug. 19, 2018
Global warming HOAX

For eons, the earth has been running hot and cold, hot and cold. Scientist, if you can believe them, tell us there have been maybe five 'ice ages' when it was very, very cold. These were followed by a warming up, getting very, very hot.

AND MAN HAD ABSOLUTELY NOTHING TO DO WITH THE HOT OR THE COLD.

Self-proclaimed Genius Al Gore, the person who invented the internet, and, also, the person who DIDNOT invent the internet, grabbed onto a Carbon Dioxide molecule, (CO_2) and scammed thousands out of millions!! The scam: Burning coal and fossil fuels to generate electricity was releasing thousands of tons of CO_2 into the atmosphere.

This increase in carbon dioxide was causing the sun's heat to be trapped and raising the global temperature at an alarming rate.

By 2006, the Arctic ice would be melted, raising the sea level by as much as 2 feet, flooding coastal cities and put New York City under water.

This was his prophecy. Mankind must slow the production CO_2 immediately, or, by 2015 the Global warming problem would be irreversible!

IT NEVER HAPPENED! ARCTIC ICE IS GREATER THAN 1996, NEW YORK CITY IS DRY AS EVER, AND SEA LEVEL CHANGE IS UNDETECTABLE.

But, never one to stop bearing a dead horse, environmentalists and global warming fanatics continue to beat their drums expounding their "Global Warming' song, only now it is CLIMATE CHANGE.

Who can argue against "Climate Change"? Happens every day and has for eons!

<u>Climate change is real. Global warming is a HOAX!</u>

Sic 'Em Donald!

Think about this. Initially, coal was the culprit. If you HAD to burn coal, you could buy $$$ "Carbon Credits". (Gore said he bought carbon credits for his 10,000 sq. ft. mansion and airplane. Yeah. You bet) Ignored were Billions of CO2 breathing humans and animals, a billion+ automobiles and trucks burning fossil fuel and generating CO2, and thousands of airplanes in the sky 24 hours a day.

I think CO2 is wonderful. Plants love it. Plants produce oxygen. I love oxygen.

Thought for the day Aug. 20, 2018
CO2 shortage

My treatise yesterday led me to learn a lot about CO2, and it is a fascinating gas.

It is essential in producing Coca Cola type drinks, making wine, preserving food, and making medicine. It is used in making plastic and many other things, including the merciful killing of hogs!

The list is very long, so I won't bore you listing more.

BUT INSTEAD OF MANKIND PRODUCING AN EXCESS AMOUNT, EUROPE AND MEXICO ARE NOW EXPERIENCING A CRITICAL SHORTAGE AND PLANTS ARE BEING SHUT DOWN.

Burn more coal!!!!

Sweltering Europe loses its fizz as CO2 shortage hits drinkers

phys.org

It's peak season for bars and barbecues in Europe as a summer heatwave coincides with the World Cup on TV. So probably not the best time for drinks companies to be running out of the gas that puts the fizz into beer and sodas. A shortage of industrial carbon dioxide (CO2) is also affecting meat ...

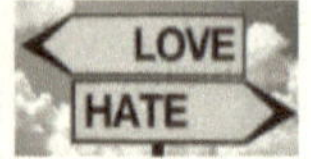

Thought for the day Aug. 21, 2018

**REMEMBER THE THOUSANDS OF 'LOVE NOT HATE' SIGNS
BEFORE NOVEMBER 9, 2016?**
Too bad. All gone. If you voted for Trump, the 'lovers' of
Hillary now hate you.
Groups like Antifa and Obama's 'shadow' army of protesters,
all hate you.
Democrat politicians all hate you.
~~LOVE NOT,~~ HATE, is marching in the streets.
But do not despair. President Trump and
60,000,000 others like you
LOVE YOU!!!!

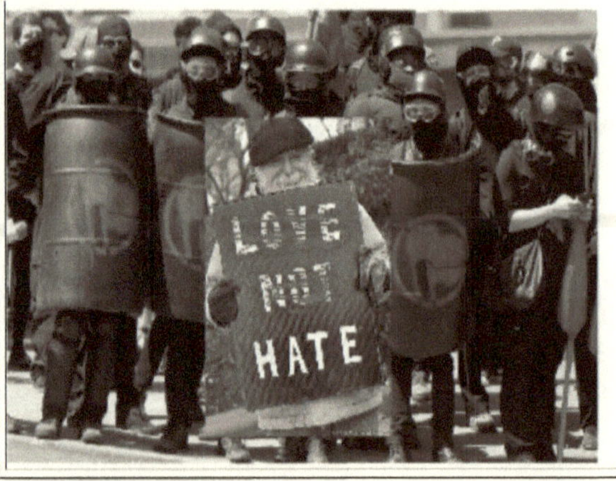

Thought for the day Aug. 22, 2018
DUMP TRUMP

Manafort guilty of 8 out of 18 charges made by Mueller. Mueller, you know, is the Special Council appointed to investigate collusion with Russia by the Trump campaign.

Finding no collusion, Mueller resigned and went back to private practice.

NO! HE DID NOT!!!

Proving 'Collusion' was just a facade. Destroy Trump. Impeach Trump was the unwritten assignment.

Muller has a reputation of being tenacious in prosecuting a case, ruining people's lives, even "knowingly" sending an innocent person to jail, just to 'win' a case.

So, where does he go from here?

Sic 'Em Donald!

The CLOSET of course. Everybody has a closet where they 'hide' things.

Paul Manafort was Trump's campaign manager for 10 days. Send the investigative dogs after Manafort. Find out what he knows about Trump's closet. When he won't talk, or lie about Trump, they go to his closet.

There, lying still, with no life, is an old charge of making money, and avoiding paying taxes.

Mueller found 18, mostly minuscule charges. This week a jury finally found him guilty of 8 out of 18, and he faces 300+ years in prison, BUT SO FAR HAS NOT LIED ABOUT TRUMP!

Not so about crooked lawyer Cohen. He is a crook, Mueller knows he is a crook.

Cohen was once Trump's lawyer. Here comes Mueller, looking in his closet! There is a thing called Attorney-client privilege. It is an evidentiary rule that protects communications between a client and his or her attorney and keeps those communications confidential.

Cohen, the crook, pleaded guilty to tax evasion, and lied about Trump, violating this rule, trying to save his own hide.

This guy planned the attack in Benghazi killing our ambassador.

He was sentenced to 22 years in prison.

SADLY, JUSTICE SEES WHAT JUSTICE WANTS TO SEE.

SIC 'EM DONALD!!!

42 – What if 'Crime'

Thought for the day Aug. 23, 2018
What if 'Crime'

Nearly two years ago, Robert Mueller was appointed Special Council.

Historically, Special Councils have been appointed to investigate a crime. Mueller was appointed with a charge to find out if the Trump campaign committed a crime.

Did the campaign "Collude" with Russia to help him win the election?

If so, would that be a crime?

Today, we know there was no collusion by Trump and NO 'crime'.

We do KNOW there was collusion by the DNC and Hillary, but there is not even a hint of investigating her Highness.

In the meantime, Mueller and his 17 investigating lawyers have long sense forgotten the original charge, AND THEY CHARGE ON!

At last count, he Mueller investigation has cost $17 million taxpayer dollars.

It has filed more than 100 criminal counts against 32 people and three companies.

But that sought after 'crime' against Trump remains allusive.

<u>The real criminal is Mueller, himself.</u>

President Trump has America to run. Problems inherited from Obama, Bush, and lover boy Clinton, are being solved by Trump working 24/7. It has become <u>blatantly</u> obvious, Mueller and the socialists Democrats are doing anything, and everything, to harass Trump, and keep him from doing his thing-MAKE AMERICA GREAT AGAIN!!!! And don't forget the Swamp Critters. Millions$$$$$ is at stake and they are still spending millions trying to save many millions!!!

SIC 'EM DONALD!!!

Trump is in a tough spot.

Try this on for size.

When I was a boy in Merkel, Texas, I had a dog named Rex. In the summer, we roamed the hills south of Merkel with my single shot 22 rifle. Sometimes I killed a jackrabbit, one time a buzzard.

One day I found a skunk in a big cactus plant.

What possessed me, I do not know, but I found a piece of barbed wire and pulled him out of the cactus.

He exercised his defense on my shoes.

The stink was stifling, and Rex and I left her.

I went home, threw my shoes in the garbage. Looking back, the stink did not bother the skunk, probably enjoyed the smell, but it cost me a pair of shoes. In a way, the situation with Trump kinda reminds me of my skunk experience.

Trump is in a tough spot. He is being squeezed from every side, hammered, threatened with impeachment and subjected to vicious lies.

Those who choose to destroy Trump, will end up like my shoes-- IN THE GARBAGE!

SIC 'EM DONALD!!!

Next

As you know a lot of my time is used in writing or thinking about writing.

Someone said to me the other day, now that you are not playing golf or bowling, writing is about all you have left. What are you going to do when you can't write anymore?

I told him I think I will lie real still in my grave.

SIC 'EM DONALD!!!

Greed

Today is Monday in Texas. Most of you know that. Those who did not know it, probably do not care what day it is. For those who thought it was Sunday, you are late for work.

For me it is just another day to write something. Last night the Dallas Cowboys tried to get in the way of the Arizona Cardinals as they raced up and down the field, BUT, with little success. Reminded me of the word 'inept'. This morning I thought about the NFL and kneeling and that led to another word 'Hypocrisy'.

Let me explain.

The NFL has no morals as we know morals. Their god is Greed. Their goal is money. Performance fills the stadium. Beating up one's wife in an elevator?

No consequences. Dragging one's wife by the hair down the street?

No consequences. Beating one's small child?

Not consequences. Spend months in rehab for drug addiction? No Consequences. Kneel for the anthem, shake your fist at the flag? No consequences.

Kneel to pray before a game like Tim Tebow? Gross!

Wear John 3:16 eye patch like Tebow? Get off the field!!! Mention or display Jesus Christ in any way? NO!NO!NO! Promote awareness for mental health, breast cancer, domestic violence, honor the BLUE, or even remember 9/11?

NO!NO!NO!

Chance for patrons to see blood spilled!! Yeah, man.

Performance is the only criteria. Satisfies GREED!

Hypocrisy in motion.

SIC 'EM DONALD!!!

Stop Trump!

With all the good things Trump has accomplished, you have to wonder why the swamp critters are so viciously intent on destroying him.

Well, you need wonder no more.

It's money! Not just money-- BIG MONEY WITH A "B"!

On March 9, 2016, before Trump was even nominated, this event occurred.

(Page 81 of "My America is Back" book)

March 9, 2016

Huffington Post reporter Ryan Grim reported that "something like 54 private jets" arrived at a private resort off the coast of Georgia with a specific focus of stopping Donald Trump from obtaining the Republican nomination for president.

Grim first reported:

Billionaires, tech CEOs and top members of the Republican establishment flew to a private island resort off the coast of Georgia.

Why? The main topic at this secretive, closed-to-the-press conference was:

How to stop Republican front-runner Donald Trump.

Some of the attendees:

Apple CEO Tim Cook, Google co-founder Larry Page,

Napster creator and Facebook investor Sean Parker,

Tesla Motors and SpaceX honcho Elon Musk,

Senate Majority Leader Mitch McConnell (R-Ky.), political guru Karl Rove,

House Speaker Paul Ryan, GOP Sens. Tom Cotton (Ark.), Cory Gardner (Colo.),

Tim Scott (S.C.), Rob Portman (Ohio) and Ben Sasse (Neb) $5,000,000 was pledged to stop Donald Trump, with a blank check for more, if needed.

(Even after being elected, the vow taken to destroy Trump continues.

After all, what is a few million to save billions!!)
SIC 'EM DONALD!!!

Thought for the day Aug. 29, 2018

I am getting sick. Sick and tired.

John McCain died last Saturday.

Today, the liberal Democrats, who hated McCain in real life, are promoting him for Sainthood.

Why? Because he hated Trump. The feeling by Trump was mutual.

What a glorious opportunity to slam Trump.

"What kind of person are you Trump who can't honor a veteran who was captured and tortured in prison for 5 years, returned home a 'hero'?"

Back up. McCain married Carol in 1965. Carol was a beautiful 5'8" swimsuit model, a divorced single mother of 2 children. McCain adopted both and they had a boy in 1966, the same year he lost his plane over Vietnam. He was captured and held in prison and tortured for 5 1/2 years, truly a horrible experience.

Unknown to John, Carol, in December of 1969 while driving alone on an icy road, crashed into a utility pole. She was thrown out of the car and laid in the snow for several hours. When found she was rushed to a hospital. She had multiple injuries-crushed legs, broken bones, ruptured spleen. After 6 months in the hospital, she was now only 5'4" tall, in a wheel chair, and overweight, no longer the swimsuit model John left in 1966. John was not told of Carol's disaster, and, of course, their reunion was a shock to him. But now John is a 'hero'. Goes everywhere, gives speeches, meets other women, yields to temptation, and marital problems develop. In 1980, he meets Cindy, 17 years younger, heir to millions, and they fall in love. John files for divorce, which was granted.

John and Cindy were married in 1981, had four children. So, today John is deceased, and Liberal Democrats who hated him while he was alive (although, at times he was one of them), now paint this glorious picture of a Trump hater.

GONE ARE the memories of poor Carol, his numerous adultery sexual encounters, his dirty mouth, and racial epithets.

On the front burner is our "terrible" President Donald J. Trump.

Makes me think of two-faced hypocrites.
SIC 'EM DONALD!!!

Thought for the day Aug. 30, 2018
Tidbits of information to remember

Trump met a few hours with Putin.

Schumer and the media accused him of treason.

Before the 2012 election, Obama sent word to Putin that he could do more for him after his reelection. in 2014, Putin took Crimea away from Ukraine.

Obama played golf. Media took a holiday.

Obama drew a red line in Syria.

Putin crossed it. Obama and media never noticed.

Hillary gave away 20% of our Uranium to Russia. Nobody even coughed when $150 million went into THE CLINTON SLUSH FUND.

For 2 years, Trump has been hampered by a Special Counsel trying to prove collusion by his campaign with Russia.

Found none.

For 2 years, everybody has known Hillary and the DNC colluded with Russia to make Hillary President. So? Hillary flits here and there, free as a bird, making speeches, and making money.

Justice is two faced.

SIC 'EM DONALD!!!

43 – Hate Clowns

Thought for the day Aug. 31, 2018
What do these pictures have in common?

KU KLUX KLAN
ANTIFA
ANTIFA
    Democrats?

THINK ABOUT IT!!!

Thought for the day Sept. 2, 2018
America today as I see it.
Today millions of us are happy, because we never had it so good. Thousands of others are bitter, unhappy, and hate those of us who are happy.
Why? Because they have never learned to trust someone, or truly feel love for someone.
In the nature of humanity, love, compassion, selflessness, require work.

    Hate requires no effort. I hate you, I hate that. Easy.

    What does "I love you" mean?

    Think about it.

    What is love? By definition " Love is love". When you find it, you just know it. It is real, and it is free. You can't buy it.

    Can you love someone who does not love you? Not really.

    I have heard people say, "I love everybody"! No, they don't.

    Can you love someone and NOT be happy? No, you can't!

    If you are happy, it shows on your face.

    If you are unhappy, you can't hide it. It, too, shows on your face.

Love is a many splendid thing, but it is also fragile.

It requires work, and tender loving care!

Happy and love are soul mates. You can't have one without the other.

Hate is a loner and it adopts Misery for a soul mate.

America, today, has millions who are happy.

Sadly, and by choice, millions are full of hate.

Hate requires no effort. Hate is like a rotting corpse.

The stink is stifling.

For me I choose to be delirious happy!!

And it is easy.

I love and am loved.

Thought for the day Sept. 3, 2018

Lonely

Yesterday I talked about Love and Happy versus Hate and Misery.

I know it sounded like an Either Love or Hate.

Not true.

In between there is LONELY.

Lonely is not happy and probably does not have a feeling of hate, Lonely is just a feeling. You can be lonely when alone or in a crowd.

Now, please understand, I am not a doctor, do not pretend to be a doctor, But I know what lonely is. I have, in my lifetime, had a feeling of loneliness and it is a dangerous feeling. Negative thoughts come easy.

I lost my first wife, Nancy, to liver cancer, following many months of suffering. After 47 years of marriage, I find myself saying "Why me, Lord? Why me?"

Then I go where the lonely go, and wrap myself in self-pity, and I cry a lot.

THEN I REMEMBER THE LORD SAID "I AM SUFFICIENT FOR YOU".

So, I said "Self, find something to do! Don't lay down!"

And the Lord provided a miracle. My high school sweetheart came back into my life.

And love turned my loneliness into happiness.

Then I lost my beautiful daughter, Pam, in 2002, to ovarian cancer, after months of suffering and I find myself saying "Why me, Lord? Why me?" And there was my sweetheart holding my hand.

Then I lost my son, Rick, this January to Vietnam war problems, after months of suffering and again, I find myself saying "Why me, Lord? Why me?" And there was my sweetheart holding my hand.

Loneliness is a curse, solved only by love.

Thought for the day Sept. 4, 2018
Hate Clowns

I wish I had something funny to say today but I do not.

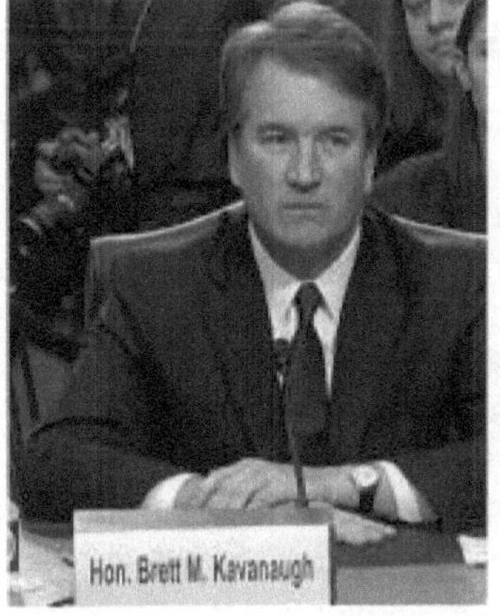

I did, however, watch about 2 hours of the Senate circus this morning. I remember going to circuses when I was younger, and also, taking my children. To me the best part was always the clowns who did silly, stupid stuff.

So far, this 'supposed to be hearing' on the confirmation of Judge Kavanaugh for the Supreme Court, has been nothing but a clown show. One set of clowns trying to make me feel good about the virtues of Judge Kavanaugh, and one set of professional clowns attacking President Trump.

Sadly, there is an utterly disgusting sideshow going on. Over the past weekend, Clown Sen. Schumer arranged for a group of Obama's PAID protesters, with professionally made signs, to attend the hearing. When a Republican started to talk, one or more started screaming profanities trying to drown out what was being said. As I am writing this, 22 have been arrested.

Sad to say, but the obvious is blatantly obvious. The Democrats are so full of hate nothing will satisfy them short of America's destruction!!

They were so crude and nasty; his wife and 3 children left the room.

THIS MAN DESERVES BETTER!
SIC 'EM DONALD!!!!

Second Thought for Sept. 4, 2018
Hate clown

A Kavanaugh hearing protester screaming obscenities while being arrested. She could have been somebody's mother, but she aborted all her chances.

There were 70 arrested today.

SIC 'EM DONALD!!!

Thought for the day Sept. 5, 2018
Really funny

It is nearly bedtime. I have been kinda brain dead all day.

Suddenly, I thought of something really funny.

Back when Obama was president, the Democrats had a majority in the Senate, but they did not have 60 votes to pass some of Obama's garbage.

Harry Reid, the Senate majority leader, you remember him. don't you? Well, to get Obama's garbage through the Senate, good old Harry managed to get the "nuclear option" passed, which changed the Senate rule requiring 60 votes for passage to a "simple majority".

At the time, Republicans thought this was a calamity.

But providence works in strange ways sometimes.

This week hearings started in the Senate, regarding the nomination of Brett Kavanaugh to the Supreme Court. The Democrats are using every device they can think of to stop his approval.

Here is where providence, and Harry Reid, prove to be a blessing.

Republicans have 51 votes, a simple majority. With Harry's "nuclear option" rule, the Democrats cannot stop him being approved.

The sound and fury of the Democrats is much ado about nothing.

Really funny how providence works. Thank you, Good Ole Harry

SIC 'EM DONALD!!!

Thought for the day Sept. 6, 2018
I COULD NOT IMPROVE ON THIS!!!

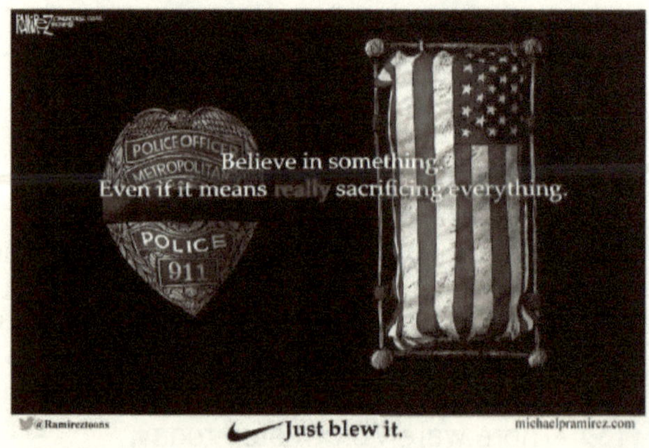

Nike signed Colin Kaepernick of NFL kneeling fame. Boycott follows. Nike just blew it! blew it! blew it!

SIC 'EM DONALD!!!

Thought for the day Sept. 7, 2018
People are different

All week I have been 'privileged' (snotty word) to witness a number of different personalities.

1. careless with the truth (liar)
2. aggravate (dispute, distort)
3. bully (shut up, I am talking)
4. actor (mouths programmed words)
5. persistent (demands one's way)
6. know it all (I am right)
7. inconsiderate (protesters)
8. Patience (Senate police)
9. Extreme patience (Kavanaugh
10. bad losers (Democrats)
11. Moderator (firm and overly fair)
12. Winners (American people)
13. NYTimes op-ed

(coward, deceitful, dishonest, untruthful, mendacious, insincere, false, disingenuous, untrustworthy, unscrupulous, unprincipled, twofaced, Janus-faced, duplicitous, double-dealing, underhanded, crafty, cunning, sly, scheming, calculating, treacherous, Machiavellian, sneaky, tricky, foxy, crooked)

SIC 'EM DONALD!!!

44 – Sept 11

Thought for the day Sept. 11, 2018

Today is 9/11, and we pause to remember a catastrophic event in our history. Two planes filled with passengers, were flown into the two World Trade center building, one plane was crashed into the Pentagon, and one crashed in a field near Shanksville, Pa.

2606 people in the World Trade Center died.

125 died at the Pentagon.

40 died at Shanksville.

343 firefighters, 72 police officers, and 55 military personnel also died. Thousands were injured. The planes were under the control of RADICAL ISLAMIC TERRORIST!!!

3 WORDS OBAMA HAS NEVER BEEN ABLE TO SAY.

The causalities at the World Trade Center and at the Pentagon were victims of being in the wrong place at the wrong time.

But Shanksville is a different story.

Flt 93 with 40 passengers and crew were headed for San Francisco.

Suddenly, passenger's phones began telling them about WTC and Pentagon.

When the plane turned back to the east, they knew their plane was hi jacked. Calmly, they developed a plan and stormed the cockpit, trying to wrest control from the 4 hijackers. Losing control, the terrorists put the plane in a dive, and it crashed in a field near Shanksville, injuring no one on the ground. Seemingly, this a simple story of bravery, but it is much more than that. It was later learned the terrorist's goal was to crash into the Capitol building, destroying it and killing hundreds more.

So, you have to ask yourself "What if..."

What if 40 brave souls had not sacrificed themselves to save many others? Sadly, but fortunately, for the Country and many other people, these 40 souls were in the right place at the right time.

Thank you.

Thought for the day Sept. 12, 2018
Niki ad????? LOVE AMERICA - Even if you must sacrifice EVERYTHING!

Thought for the day Sept. 13, 2018
BUILD THE WALL!!

I saw this headline about Bangladeshi Nationals, and I got curious.

"100 Bangladeshi Nationals apprehended near Texas Border in 3 weeks." These people are not Mexican or Hispanic.

Where on earth is Bangladesh?

I found it bordering on India, 8500 miles ACROSS THE PACIFIC OCEAN from Texas!

Its size is about 58,000 sq. miles and has a population density of 2700!!! people per sq. mile. That compares to Texas with a density of

105!! people/sq. mile. As of this date, 622 Bangladeshis have crossed the border in 2018, compared to 161 in 2017.

Considering the population density and the poverty in Bangladesh, it is easy to understand why a person would want to leave. But why the big increase now? How do they get from Bangladesh to Mexico? Border patrol says they pay a Cartel about $27,000 each, to be smuggled into the USA.

Unlike most illegals, they do not hide or try to escape.

They walk right up to an agent and claim 'credible fear'.

This raises a serious question about our border with NO WALL. If illegals can get here from 8500 miles away, they can come from anywhere, and be any kind of person. Do we pay to send them back to their country, or jail them, or put them on Food Stamps and let them loose on the country?

Or do you................

BUILD THE WALL!!! SIC 'EM DONALD!!!

Thought for the day Sept. 14, 2018
Despicable

Hurricane Florence has been promising to hit the Carolina's for over a week.

Today, it has kept its promise and is making a real mess. Over 40" of rain and still raining. Over a million people without power, and several hundred begging to be rescued.

(Florence caught them by surprise. "Nobody told us!") Elsewhere in this crazy world, we have politicians who, also, are full of surprises.

Democrats are so desperate to stop the confirmation of Judge Kavanaugh, they are resorting to despicable stuff. Yesterday, Sen. Diane Feinstein said this "I have received information from an individual concerning the nomination of Brett Kavanaugh to the Supreme Court," Ms. Feinstein said in a statement. "That individual strongly requested confidentiality, declined to come forward or press the matter further, and I have honored that decision."

??? ...."honored that decision".??? What is 'honor' to her? She just told the whole world and turned it over to investigative authorities.

Supposedly, she has had this 'letter' since July and, only now, with Kavanaugh' nomination imminent, does she disclose this 'secret' information, about a 'secret' event 40 years ago in Kavanaugh's life, from an anonymous person, who requests to remain anonymous.

This old dog won't hunt anymore. During the Election

Sic 'Em Donald!

Democrats dug up imaginary stuff on Trump from 30-40 years ago, and poor old Roy Moore got destroyed by a 40-year-old imaginary event in his life. Despicable!

SIC 'EM DONALD!!!

Thought for the day Sept. 17, 2018

Test your detective skills

THIS IS SOMETHING DIFFERENT. IT IS A TEST OF YOUR IMAGINATION. <u>HOWEVER THERE IS NO FAILING GRADE.</u>

Imagination is funny. Once you start imagining about something, your mind can run off in all directions.

For instance, two people were killed recently in totally unrelated incidents.

In case #1, <u>a white woman police officer shot</u> and <u>killed a black man.</u>

In the second case, <u>a black man shot</u> and <u>killed a white police officer</u>.

In case one, the police woman is charged with manslaughter of a black person she thought was a burglar in her apartment, <u>which was not her apartment</u>. A terrible mistake.

The victim was 26 years old, a college graduate with a very good job.

Apparently, a good citizen.

Protest marches have started in the streets.

<u>Question:</u> How do you imagine this will end?

In case #2, <u>Three young black men</u> were robbing a store.

Police caught them in the act.

Gunfire erupted.

One of the young black men<u> killed a white officer,</u> and he, was subsequently killed by another officer.   The <u>other two men were arrested and charged with assault, armed robbery, and accessory to murder.</u> The white officer had served 17 years on the police force and had saved numerous lives. The police force lost a Hero!

He was married with two daughters.

Question: How do you imagine this will end?

If this interest you or makes you curious, THINK ABOUT IT.

Otherwise, feel free to hit the 'delete' button.

Thought for the day Sept. 18, 2018
The Kavanaugh saga

- Early July: secret letter with secret content by anonymous person shows up in Sen. Feinstein's office.
- Mid-July: Feinstein forwards letter to FBI. FBI "No comment".
- Late July: Anonymous secret person takes a secret lie detector test, administered by ex-FBI agent. Results unknown.
- August: Confirmation hearings conducted on Judge Kavanaugh. Secret person secretly contacted by Washington Post, arch enemy of President Trump. Secret person then secretly hires high-priced lawyer. (Is the Post paying the lawyer and the secret person/)
- Sept. 13: One week before conformation is scheduled to be voted on, Feinstein reveals receipt and content of secret letter received in July. Letter claims Kavanaugh molested her 35 or 36 years ago, when she was 15 or 16, in 1982 or 1983. Can't remember for sure. Supposedly, she was at a party in a private residence, and everybody was drinking beer. She admits to having one beer, but she doesn't know how she got home?
- (Suddenly, you have to wonder why Feinstein, after days of   open hearings on Judge Kavanaugh, and an hour of one-on-one   with the Judge, chose to reveal the letter and person at this time.) Wonder no longer. This is the Democrat Socialist MO.

A little history.

In 1991, Clarence Thomas, a black man, politically conservative, was nominated by Pres. George H.W. Bush, a Republican, to the Supreme Court. Suddenly, Anita Hill, a black woman, who had worked for Thomas, came forth claiming he had harassed her. Despite her CHARGE, he was confirmed, and today is one of our best Justices.

But yesterday, yes, YESTERDAY, 9.17 this happened:

Matthew Dowd, the chief political analyst for ABC News, smeared

Supreme Court Justice Clarence Thomas with a "sexual predator" allegation on Monday.

(actually, by inference, comparing Thomas to Kavanaugh)

Fast forward from 1991 to October 2016, 3 weeks before election day-Trump vs Clinton. Suddenly, a 75-year-old grandmother comes forward, claiming Trump molested her on an airplane in 1985 while riding in 1st class with Trump.

Democrats and media pulled out all the stops to make sure Hillary won.

Democrat MO. Didn't work.

Now it is today. Dr. Christine Ford, an admitted Socialist Democrat with a fuzzy memory, and mental problems, but active imagination, has laid herself on the Democrat altar in an attempt to deny Bret Kavanaugh the nomination for Supreme Court Judge.

Democrat MO. This old DOG won't hunt!

SIC 'EM DONALD!!! WE GOT TO HAVE BRETT!!!

2nd Thought Sept. 18, 2018
Kavanaugh Saga, Page 2

Kavanaugh's accuser, Dr. Christine Ford, sent a secret letter to Sen. Feinstein detailing sexual assault 36 years ago.

Initially, she insisted on remaining anonymous, but she, for some reason, took a lie detector test, the results of which are not known.

Next, she talks to the Washington Post, Trump's enemy. Then she hires a high-priced lawyer, paid for by whom? Finally, she comes forward, citing it is her civic duty to let the world know what happened to her when she was about 15 or 16 (can't remember exactly).

Now that she has threatened to tell her story, under oath, she suddenly disappears. Her lawyer won't respond to inquiries. Even Feinstein is wavering about the validity of her story. Frankly, I think this an attempted hatchet job by the DSA,

(Democrat Socialist Assn), trying to ruin a good person's life.

It is the same MO used to destroy Roy Moore in Mississippi.

last year.

45 – Sometimes We are the Toilet

Thought for the day Sept. 20, 2018
Sometimes we are the toilet

It happens to everyone now and then, but too often for President Trump. And now Kavanaugh!!

SIC 'EM DONALD!!!

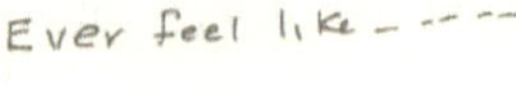

What is wrong with this picture?

THOUGHT FOR THE DAY SEPT. 21, 2018
KAVANAUGH SAGA continues
Summary of Dr. Ford to date

Wrote secret letter about secret event to Sen. Feinstein.
Request anonymity.
Went to Wash. Post, spilled secret.
Had lie detector test.
Hired high-price woman lawyer.
Feinstein shares secret with world.
Dr. Ford agrees to testify before Congress.
Dr. Ford changes mind.
Dr. Ford changes mind. Kavanaugh has to testify first.

Dr. Ford will then testify WITHOUT Kavanaugh in room. (See picture above) Nuts!

Meanwhile, bio of Dr. Ford seeps out, bit by bit.

Promiscuous comes to mind.

After high school, worked summers as a waitress in a bar at Dewey Beach.

(Check internet "Dewey Beach in the 1980's)
"Dewey Beach: Grownups gone wild"

'Dewey Beach is where Washington singles-young and old-   go to relax, drink, and find true love. Or at least a one-night stand'.

Questions about her life on Dewey Beach, 'might' be embarrassing.

Following College graduation Dr. Ford went to California to stay. Around 1988, she moved in with Russell Biddle Ford, who she eventually married fourteen years later in 2002. They have two children.

TODAY, SHE AND HER LAWYER, KATZ, ARE DOING EVERYTHING THEY CAN TO PREVENT HER FROM TESTIFYING.

Do you wonder why?

Promiscuous comes to mind.

SIC 'EM DONALD!!!

Thought for the day Sept. 22, 2018
Kavanaugh-Ford Fiasco

Dr. Ford told The Post she did not recall exactly who owned the house, how she came to be at the house, or how the gathering was arranged. She remembered only that the house was in Montgomery County, near a country club, and that parents were not present.

Read this carefully.

Ford claimed she was assaulted. There are no witnesses.

It happened in a house. Location unknown.

Who owned the house? Does not know.

How did she get there? Does not remember.

Why was she there? Can't remember.

House was somewhere in Montgomery County. Really?

4 boys, or maybe 3, maybe just 2 boys and one girl present. Not sure.

Had one beer. Maybe more?

Made her drunk? very possible.

Accused assault described in minute detail. Can't remember anything else.

Doesn't know how she got home.

Told no one until now, 36 years later.
Agreed to testify, BUT <u>she is afraid to fly</u>.
Must drive.
How did she get to Washington, DC to talk to Wash. Post? Drove?
How did she find her DC lawyer?
Did she fly or drive back to California? Guess.
She is now stalling on testifying. Why?
She was so eager to bare her soul with the letter.
2nd thoughts? Are there skeletons in her closet? apparently!!! Is she lying? Is this revenge for a ruling made against   her parents by Judge Kavanaugh's Mother?
Why did she visit a shrink in 2012? Why? Why?
Sad. The Democrats, in their desperation to block Dr. Kavanaugh are placing Dr. Ford on the sacrificial altar. It matters not what her life will be like after the blood is spilled.
But it will never be the same, nor will she be happy.
Probably will stay in close touch with that 2012 doctor.
Name of the game now>>>>STALLING.

Thought for the day Sept. 24, 2018
CRAZY

Kavanaugh- Ford-Ramirez-Who's next

The hate demonstrated by the Democrat Socialist party for Trump, Kavanaugh, and America, is gut wrenching!

Why? Under Obama they had made so much progress toward converting America into another Venezuela. Now Trump is trying, through his nominee Kavanaugh, to make our Supreme Court a constitutional court, instead of a Progressive Court.

So, they set out to destroy anyone Trump nominates, qualifications be damned!!

Let us see where we are.

DNC MO. Find woman. Accuse nominee of sexual harassment. Case 1. Dr. Ford, recruited. Swears she was harassed at a party 35 maybe 36 years ago. Not sure how she got to party, not sure where it was, not sure who was there, had been drinking, might have been drunk, hazy on everything, but sure of harassment event by accused, <u>and has no idea how she got home!!!</u>(Who can dispute

"facts" like this) Hires 3 lawyers, paid for by DNC, to help put the right words in her mouth. 'May' testify Sept. 27, 2018.

Case 2. Find woman. Accuse nominee of sexual harassment.

Sic 'Em Donald!

'Found' Deborah Ramirez, age 53, who was a 19-year-old freshman at Yale 35 years ago, who <u>claims</u> she went to a party in a dormitory room where a lot of drinking was going on. She became totally incapacitated, drunk, (Her own words) and on the floor, foggy and slurring her words.

While in this state, she said some man exposed himself to her.

She did not know who it was, or for sure it happened.

But after 6 days of coaching by her DNC paid lawyer, she experienced a miracle and she can now recall, in vivid terms, detail what happened. However, neither the Democrats nor the New York Times have been able to find any collaborating witnesses, after interviewing about 20 possibilities. So, nobody knows what happened, except Ramirez, AND SHE DOES NOT KNOW EITHER!!!

Watching this unfold as the Democrats are now in the process of destroying two women and using them in an attempt to destroy Judge Kavanaugh, you have to wonder why a decent person would join the Democrat politicians in the sewer.

CRAZY

46 – Kavanaugh Hearings

Thought for the day Sept. 26, 2018
California's blessed Millionaires

Nancy Pelosi   **Diane Feinstein**

Nancy Pelosi, age 78. Has been on public payroll her entire working life.

Currently, very Liberal minority leader House of Representatives. Represents San Francisco.

Salary $ 193,400/mo.

Current worth $101,000,000!!!!

What do I think when I see her?

Some of my tax money goes to make this 'bimbo' rich.

Diane Feinstein, age 85. Has been on public payroll for the last 52 years.

Currently extreme Liberal Senator from California.

Salary $ 193,400

Current worth $100,000,000 ++!!!!

What do I think when I see her?

Conniving, dishonest, unscrupulous, rich old woman.

QUESTION: Did you ever wonder how they got so rich?
.............just asking.

Thought for the day Sept. 27, 2018

The hearing to be

I have watched the attempted lynching of Judge Kavanaugh with disgust since the obvious became obvious!! It was known before Trump nominated Kavanaugh that Democrats would oppose ANYONE he nominated. At the last moment when Kavanaugh's approval seemed imminent, the Democrats drag out Dr. Ford with her claim of being sexually assaulted 36 years ago.

This was just before a vote was to be taken.

A serious allegation, when she was 15 years-old -36 years ago! Turns out she hates President Trump, has marched in protest against him, and is friends with George Soros, who is dedicated to destroying America, also a promoter of Obama and Hillary.

There are no witnesses to the "assault"!

So, dirt was thrown in works, and Republicans agreed to hear her story.

Supposedly, that will be tomorrow, Thursday, IF she shows up.

Next comes Deborah Ramirez with a similar story, everybody drunk.

Debbie was falling down drunk, had vague memory, but after spending 6 days with her lawyer, the lawyer was able to fill in the 'gaps', and "knows" her molester was Kavanaugh!!

BUT no witnesses.

This week Porn lawyer Avanetti finds Julie Swetnick with a story which really stretches the imagination. She is 2 years older than Kavanaugh and had graduated from high school. She was 19 years-old when the event occurred, 36 years ago.

As her story goes, she attended at least 10 drinking parties where one girl was selected to have sex with multiple partners. We do not know why she kept going back to these high school parties, knowing what was going on. Apparently, she was disappointed she was not picked, so, she kept going back. Finally, it was her turn.

Again, there are no witnesses.

Democrat POWER will be diminished considerably with Kavanaugh on the Court. They play dirty. Anything goes. Sacrificing 3 or more women to save their power is a small price to pay!

SIC 'EM DONALD!!!

THOUGHT FOR THE DAY OCT. 1, 2018

THE FARCE

Why not investigate Ford? Why is she getting a free ride? She told several lies.

What was her life like from 1982 till she got married 20 years later? How many more beer parties did she go to?

How many more "molestations" did she incur?

Did Mr. Ford marry a virgin? Just wondering.

THE CLAUSTROPHOBIC LIE

Dr. Ford, in her testimony Thursday, Sept. 27, claimed she suffers from claustrophobia.

For that reason, she was afraid to fly because you are so confined, and there is no escape. Lie, she flies many times every year! During her testimony, she claimed that after her visit to the shrink for mental problems in 2012, they had a second door installed in their house.

Why? to give her, in an emergency, another escape route.

Perjury!! Pictures of her house in 2007 show ONE door. Pictures of her house in 2011 show TWO doors. So, the shrink visit, and claustrophobia, had nothing to do with the 2nd door. Records indicate a small business, in 2012, used the same physical address as the house. Why?

Plus, during the shrink visit, Kavanaugh's name was not mentioned. Years later,

- (like this summer), her husband said she told him the un-named molester was Kavanaugh.

THE LIE DETECTOR LIE

After hiring two Democrat lawyers (recommended by Diane Feinstein), she took a lie detector "test" which was as follows: Wrote out description of assault in handwriting.

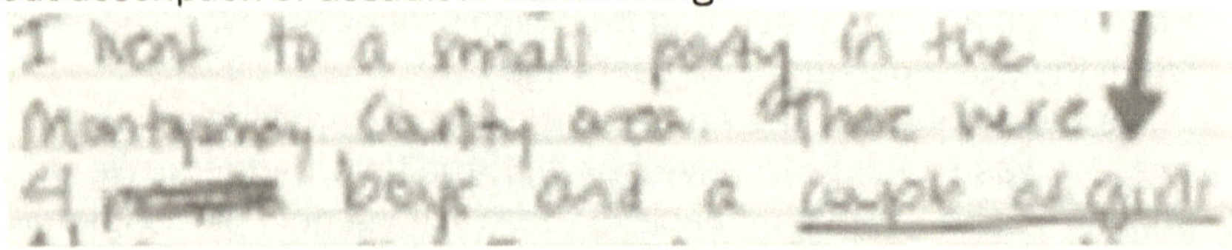

Her scribbling. Dr Ford was then asked two questions: "Is any part of your statement false?" and "Did you make up any part of your statement?" TWO QUESTIONS!

IN HER TESTIMONY, SHE SAID SHE WAS ASKED MANY QUESTIONS.

THOUGHT FOR THE DAY OCT. 2, 2018

Disgusting.

Julie Swetnick said she was gang raped and accused Bret Kavanaugh of being one of the participants. She lied.

Some dirty facts.

She admitted attending ten (10) gang rape parties.

She admitted she was finally the Star of a party!!

She accused Brett of sexual assault.
Correction: Cannot definitely say he did.
She said she saw Brett spiking drinks of women.
Correction: She saw Brett near the punch bowl.

She is represented by Porn lawyer Avanti, a dirt bag. Her ex-boyfriend (7 years) says she is a known liar, is unscrupulous, mentally unstable, and once, for spite, threatened to kill their unborn child.

Finally, she dropped this 'gem':

"It's very hard for me to talk about this, but it's important that somebody says something, because **if** Brett Kavanaugh was one of those people that did this to me, there is no way in the world that he should go scot-free on this, and that he should be on the Supreme Court," Swetnick added.

"It's just unthinkable to me. If he does, there's no justice in the world." In the interview, she also named four people who allegedly went to these "gang rape" parties with her — but none of them were able to corroborate her story.

One denied knowing anything about it. One is dead. Two not heard from.

Sick. Trying to destroy a person with an "**if**".

DISGUSTING!!!

Thought for the day Oct. 3,
Liar, Liar

ON MAY 27, 2010 THIS ARTICLE APPEARED IN THE NEW YORK TIMES. BLUMENTHAL LIVED OFF HIS fictitious VIETNAM SERVICE FOR 12 YEARS, UNTIL HE WAS CAUGHT IN HIS LIE. THEN, HE SAID HE DID NOT LIE.

'HE MISSPOKE'!!!! For 12 years!!!!!!??????
And the difference is................?
Now he is trying to crucify Kavanaugh!

Chang W. Lee/The New York Times May 27, 2010

A CANDIDATE FOR THE SENATE
Mr. Blumenthal at an April forum in Monroe. He is running for the seat Christopher J. Dodd is vacating.

He served in the Marine Reserve.

"We have learned something important since the days <u>that I served in Vietnam,"</u> Mr. Blumenthal said to the group gathered in Norwalk in March 2008. There was one problem: Mr. Blumenthal, a Democrat <u>now running for the United States Senate</u>, never served in Vietnam.

He obtained at least five military deferments from 1965 to 1970 and took repeated steps that enabled him to avoid going to war, according to records.

In 2003, he addressed a rally in Bridgeport, where about 100 military families gathered to express support for American troops overseas. <u>"When we returned</u>, we saw nothing like this," Mr. Blumenthal said. "Let us do better by this generation of men and women."

"I served during the Vietnam era," he said. "I remember the taunts, the insults, sometimes even physical abuse." Scumbag! (My word) LIAR!

Thought for the day Oct. 4, 2018
DEMOCRATS VS AMERICA

Who will win this Supreme Court debacle?

It appears to me, if Kavanaugh is confirmed, America wins and everybody else loses.

If Kavanaugh is not confirmed, nobody wins.

Oh yeah, Democrats will gloat with glee because their goal of Destruction was achieved.

But destroying America is NOT a win.

Think about this.

Confirm or not confirm, unproven allegations, lies, and deception, have destroyed the Kavanaugh family, fomented hate, and turned friends into forever enemies.

This debacle will haunt America for many years, maybe forever.

The Democrats may have just turned off the "LIGHT ON THE HILL". The Supreme Court is charged with correctly applying our Constitution to laws passed by Congress. The nine members should be well versed in law and neutral politically. (Sadly, they are not neutral).

SO, I have said all of this to say this:

"Who, in their right mind, would volunteer to submit

themselves to character assignation like this circus has been?" Answer: No One. (Can you imagine a Supreme Court filled with idiots like we have on Congress?) Finally, a word about Dr. Ford.

Things we know.

She is a Trump hater. Participated in a 'Dump Trump" protest march.

Sic 'Em Donald!

Has a mental problem. Told many lies in her testimony.

Could not remember something she said or did a month ago. Lived with a 'boyfriend' for at least 6 years. Had consensual sex with others. Her lawyers are strong Democrat supporters recommended by none other than Sen. Diane Feinstein.

What we do not know.

If she went to beer drinking parties at 15, and slept with an unknown number of men, before marrying twenty years later, in 2002, did she really have a 'terrifying' experience like she described? Obviously, IF she did, she got over IT years ago!!

47 – Light on the Hill

Thought for the day Oct. 5,
Actions have consequences

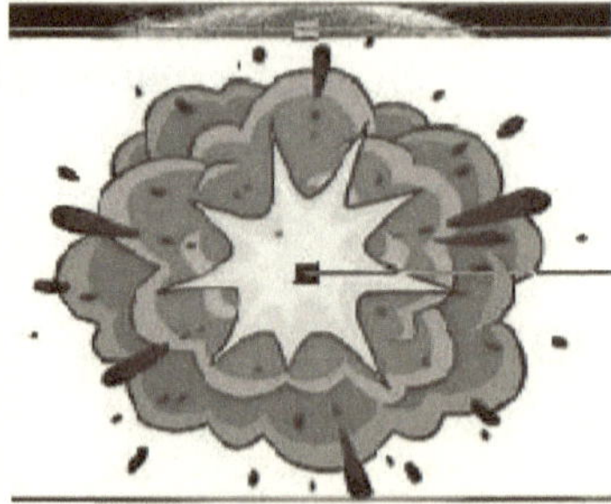

I say this, not with disrespect, just the respect she is due. "O". This is Sen. Diane Feinstein, an 85-year-old woman, who looks older today, whose cleverly concocted and vicious scheme to defeat the nomination of Brett Kavanaugh for the Supreme Court has blown up in her face!!

The best laid plans of mice, men, old women, AND CROOKED politicians often go astray.

THANK GOODNESS!

Thought for the day Oct. 7, 2018
Thank you, LORD!

Dallas Morning News
DALLASNEWS.com
Dallas, Texas, Sunday, October 7, 2018

SUPREME COURT

Kavanaugh confirmed

Conservative narrowly wins approval after bruising partisan battle

FROM WIRE REPORTS

WASHINGTON — The Senate confirmed Brett Kavanaugh as the 114th Supreme Court justice on Saturday by one of the narrowest margins in history, ending a vitriolic battle over his nomination and conservative ma-

BRETT KAVANAUGH

As a throng of angry demonstrators stood on the steps of the Capitol, the Senate finalized on a near party-line vote of 50-48 what will certainly be one of President Donald Trump's most enduring legacies: two Supreme Court justic- an increas-

ingly polarized nation.

Kavanaugh was later sworn in by Chief Justice John Roberts and retired Justice Anthony Kennedy — the court's long-time swing vote, whom he will replace — in a private ceremony.

The brutal confirmation fight is likely to have far-reaching implications in next month's midterm elections. Republicans are confronting an electrified Democratic base led by women infuriated by the

treatment of Christine Blasey Ford, who detailed in emotional testimony her allegations that Kavanaugh sexually assaulted her when both were teenagers. Kavanaugh has denied the allegations.

Yet Republicans say the battle to get Kavanaugh confirmed — in the face of Democratic opposition and the "mob" of Kavanaugh demonstrators who flooded the Capi-

See KAVANAUGH

WHAT A WONDERFUL DAY FOR AMERICA!

Thought for the day Oct. 8, 2018
Light on the hill

As we journey through life, the road we travel has many forks.

At each one, a decision must be made.

Do I go right? Do I go left?

Once you choose, there is no turning back.

Each decision becomes a learning experience. Today, because of the many decisions we have made, we are what we are, like it or not.

America is like that. Decisions over the years have made America what it is (or was). America became a "Light on the Hill", A kind of paradise, envied by the World.

In 2008, EMOTION made a decision to elect Obama President. It seemed so right but is was so wrong. The "Light" began to fade.

WE learned a little, but not very much! In 2012, EMOTION re-elected Obama, compounding the wrong!

By 2016, we are now smart, but the "light" is going out!

Faced with staying on the road to <u>Venezuela</u>, or

Restoring America's glory, America chose Trump. What a blessing it has been. Thank you, Lord. For the last 3 months, America has been at a fork facing a decision, to approve or disapprove Judge Kavanaugh for the Supreme Court.

Experience and common sense prevailed, and he is now Associate Justice of the Supreme Court of the United States!!! SCOTUS! The "Light" has been turned back on.

SIC 'EM DONALD!!!

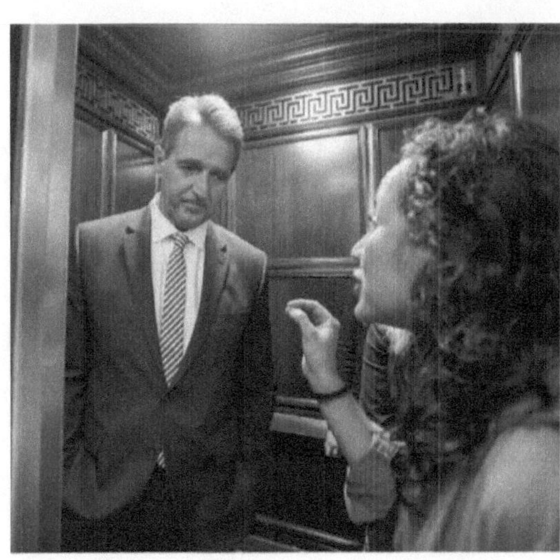

Thought for the day Oct. 9, 2018
Remember this picture?

Is it Sen. Flake being viciously dressed down by a victim of sexual assault? Touches your heart, right? Poor woman! Who is this bitter soul?

Well, guess what? It ain't what you think. In a pivotal moment,

Ana Maria Archila, <u>co-executive director of the Center for Popular Democracy,</u> cornered Sen. Jeff Flake, Arizona Republican, in an elevator and criticized Justice Kavanaugh. Made Jeff feel bad.

Who is this Ana Maria Archila?

Ana was born in Columbia. Came to America when 17.

Got a job as a Community Organizer (Obama's Clan).

Worked her way up to be <u>co-executive director of the Center for Popular Democracy.</u> What is the CPD? Turns out it is a <u>very organized Protest group,</u> with many chapters around the US.

CPD is a part of Obama's 'Shadow government', financed by George Soros, which is spending millions to recruit Protesters and destroy America.

Note Ana's salary WAS $178,071 in 2016. Probably more now.

Ana hates Trump, Kavanaugh, and America. Her foul-mouthed screeching had nothing to do with "Sexual Assault".

It was designed to kill Kavanaugh's nomination, AND IT ALMOST WORKED! Trump was right. We have well-paid protesters, who recruit 'suckers' to protest for nothing.

CPD is a cancer and spreading. Sadly, many lives have been negatively impacted by this ugly, vicious, shameless, down -in-the-dirt conformation process of now, thankfully, JUSTICE BRETT KAVANAUGH!!

SIC 'EM DONALD!!

Thought for the day Oct. 10, 2018

SEXUAL ASSAULT

I am not a doctor, but I know some things doctors know.

I am not wise in psychiatry, but I know something about people.

Sometimes I go where no man should go. This is one of those times. For the past few weeks the country has been inundated with sexual assault of women, and men, all men, have been castigated, and are guilty by accusation.

Let us try to be adults as we exam this subject.

GOD created <u>every</u> living thing with a SEX drive to reproduce, and with humans, in their reproductive years, this 'Drive' is difficult to control. When God's rules are violated, <u>debauchery results.</u>

Examples: A woman, fully clothed, is caught unawares, and assaulted.

Man's fault. (This is the bad one. Involves sick person)

A woman, partially clothed, teases a man with inviting gestures. Assaulted.

Man accused. Woman's fault.
Mutual consent. No fault.
Mutual consent. Man accused. Vengefully charged. Woman's fault.
Imaginary assault. Man blamed. Woman's fault.
Woman's advances spurned. Man charged falsely. Woman's fault.
Score: Men 1, Women 5, tie 1
Today, sex, or imagined sex, is flaunted everywhere.
"If it feels good, do it!"
Now, about Judge Kavanaugh................................ From the beginning, our justice system has been: the accused is presumed Innocent until proven guilty. I have always wondered why, when a person commits a crime, and he is caught in the act, the report is given "Suspect in custody".

"Innocent until proven guilty." I have said all of this, to say this:
Everyone who found Kavanaugh guilty, "BY HER SAY SO", without any proof, and is without sin, are invited to my 'Rock throwing party'.
I will furnish the rocks.
Finally, I am not guilty of anything you may accuse me of!
I am 93 today and I DON'T CARE!!!!!

SIC 'EM DONALD!!!

Thought for the day Oct. 11, 2018
Why the hate?

You see what is happening today with riots, Antifa and other protests, like the one around Kavanaugh's nomination process.

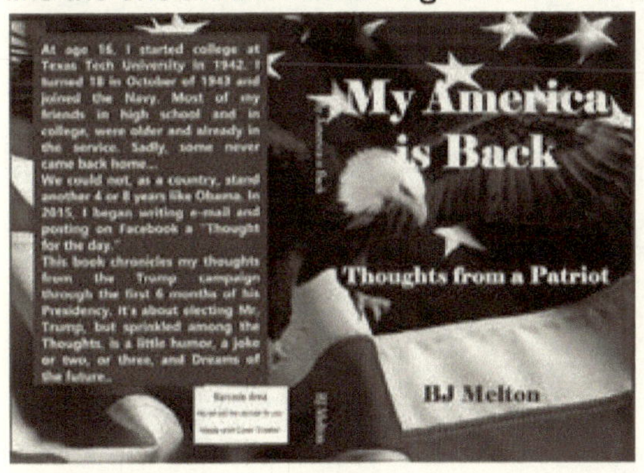

You see the hate and hear the hateful rhetoric condemning President Trump and Kavanaugh.
It is nasty, demeaning and destructive.
You may be asking "Why is this happening?"
It is happening because it was planned to happen by Obama and George Soros!!!!!

The reason is covered in my book "My America is back".
If you really want to know, read pages: 342, 355, 356, 400, 446, 447.

SIC 'EM DONALD!!!

Thought for the day Oct. 13, 2018
This is WAR!

VANDALS HIT NYC GOP HEADQUARTERS: 'ATTACK IS MERELY A BEGINNING'

Kerry Picket | Reporter   1:34 PM 10/12/2018 | US

Thursday night the Metropolitan Republican Club was vandalized by the leftist hate group Antifa, who also left a note promising 'this is just the beginning' and threatening more violence,"

Tonight, we put the Republican Party on notice, our attack is merely a beginning. We are not passive, we are not civil, and we will not apologize. This is WAR in our time!!!

We can no longer stick our heads up our rear! This is WAR. These hooded vandals are showing up all over the country, destroying property, intimidating and molesting young and old people alike. This is not protesting for "rights", it is MOB RULE! It is Obama's Community organizers gone bezerk!

It is part of his plan to destroy our government and America. It is promoted and paid for by George Soros and Obama and claiming their right to protest under the "FREE SPEECH" guarantee of the 1st Amendment. Legal protest is one thing, MOB RULE is not legal. It is WAR.

Somehow it must be squashed before it consumes our country.
TIME TO SIC 'EM DONALD!!!

48 – Election Day

Thought for the day Oct. 17, 2018
VOTE NOVEMBER 6!!!!!!!!!!!!!!

DEMOCRAT SOCIALIST THUGS

DEMOCRAT SOCIALIST 'LADY'?

GIMME!!!!
BETO SOCIALIST!!!

"GET IN THEIR FACE DEMOCRAT"

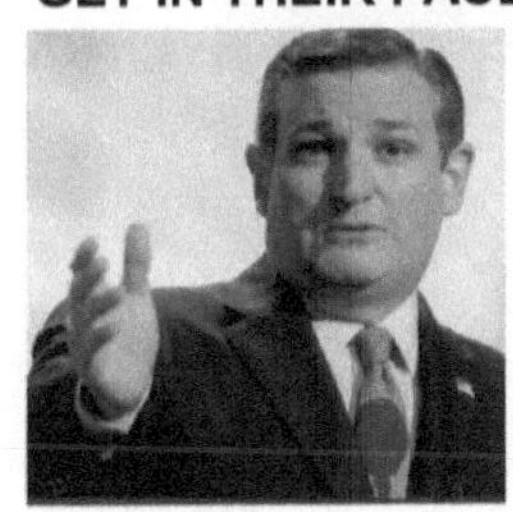

TED CRUZ, CONSERVATIVE

DO YOU REALLY HAVE A CHOICE?

VOTE NOVEMBER 6!!!!!!!!!!!!!!!!!

Thought for the day Oct. 19, 2018
Guilty throwing rocks!
I find this picture extremely interesting.
On the left is Sen. Mazie Hirono from Hawaii. During the Kavanaugh hearings, continually voiced her hate for Kavanaugh and men in general.

Quote: she told the "men of this country to shut up and step up for once" Babbles like an idiot.

In the middle, is none other than Sen. Elizabeth Warren, from Massachusetts. For most of her life she has claimed to be part Indian and took full advantage of benefits awarded to 'minorities'.

She lied!

She ain't no minority, but she is in the majority of Democrats who lie.

Also babbles like an idiot.

Finally, on the right is none other than Sen. Richard Blumenthal, from Connecticut. For years he claimed to be a Vietnam veteran, who suffered the horrors of war, and his unwelcome back home.

He lied.

He never left Connecticut. Found ways to dodge the draft.

Made a living playing on the sympathies of good people.

Said "I didn't lie. I misspoke".

He lied.

And being a lying Democrat, he had the gall and audacity to find Kavanaugh GUILTY, not for what he did or didn't do, but because Trump nominated him.

Babbles like an idiot.

DO YOU WANT THESE PEOPLE MAKING THE RULES YOU HAVE TO PLAY WITH?

If not, Vote November 6!!!

SIC 'EM DONALD!!!

Thought for the Day Oct. 20, 2018
The invasion

With the horde of immigrants headed this way, ingenuity created this bumper sticker.

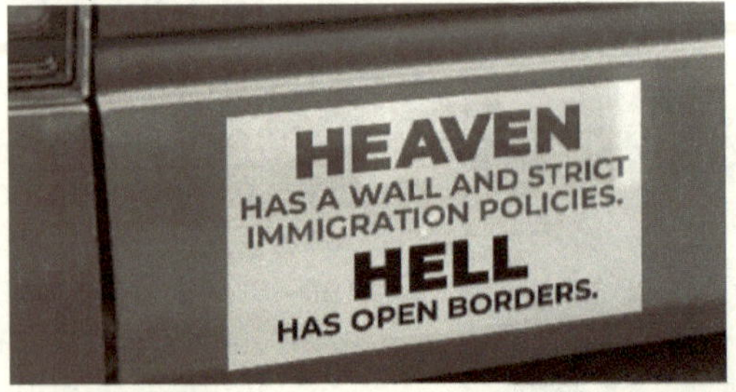

Paul Revere rode through the streets of Boston yelling "The Redcoats are coming. The Redcoats are coming!"

President Trump is on Twitter yelling "Build the wall! Build the Wall!

SIC 'EM DONALD!!!

Thought for the day Oct. 22, 2018

THE WEDDING

It was to be a marriage made in Heaven.

The mother of the bride was weeping with joy.

The father of the groom was so proud of his only son.

The congregation was filled with happiness for the beautiful couple. It was a beautiful, wondrous event.

The wedding ceremony came to the point where the minister asked if anyone had anything to say concerning the union of the bride and groom. A beautiful young woman in the back of the congregation, stood up, carrying a child.

She started walking slowly down the aisle towards the minister.

You could hear the gasps for breath and feel the shock of disbelief!

Deathly silence fell on the congregation. You could hear a pin drop.

The groom was stunned, his jaw dropped.

He stood dumbfounded, watching the approaching young woman and child.

Chaos ensued.

The bride burst out crying, threw her bouquet into the air, and screamed obscenities at the groom.

The groom's mother fainted.

The best men started giving each other looks and wondering how to save the situation.

The minister, striving to remain calm, asked the woman, "Can you tell us, young lady, why you have come forward?

Do you have something to say?"

The silent anticipation was smothering.

The woman replied, "We could not hear you in the back."

See what happens when people are considered guilty UNTIL PROVEN INNOCENT!!!!

Sound familiar? Remember Kavanaugh?

SIC 'EM DONALD!!!

Thought for the day Oct. 23, 2018

Here are 26 Democrats

Who would like the rules for you

Starting in 2020

22 of them want to be your President!!!

You may not know some of them now, but by 2020,

you will know some very, very, well!

SIC 'EM DONALD!!!

Thought for the day Oct. 24, 2018
Democrat MO: Method of Operation

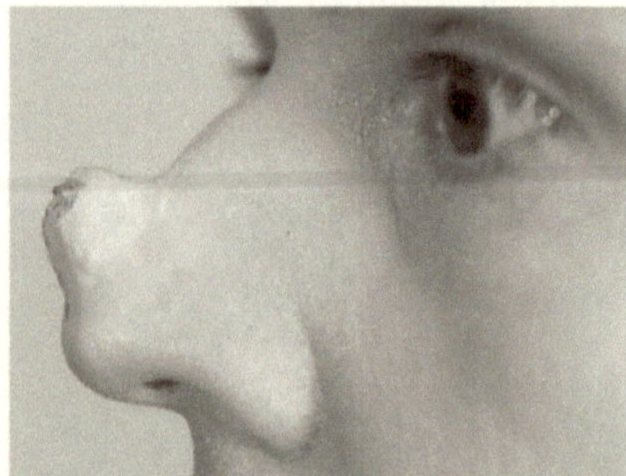

As obvious as.... a wart on your nose. Falsely accuse Trump guilty of Russia collusion. Obvious lie Falsely accuse Trump of Tearing babies from mothers' arms. Obvious lie. Lying Dr. Ford. Obvious Destroy Judge Kavanaugh & family. Obvious New caravan from Mexico. Obvious Bombs sent to Socialist Democrats. Obvious Will do anything to destroy President Trump! Obvious. Democrat MO: Obvious - IT AIN'T WORKING!!!

SIC 'EM DONALD!!!

Thought for the day Oct. 25, 2018

Repeat lies, over and over

You have to understand the creed of Communists. Rule # 1: Accuse others of doing the things of which YOU are guilty.

"President Trump's words ring hollow until he reverses his statements that condone acts of violence.

Time and time again, the President has condoned physical violence and divided Americans with his words and his actions: expressing support for the Congressman who body-slammed a reporter, the neo-Nazis who killed a young woman in Charlottesville, his supporters at rallies who get violent with protesters, dictators around the world who murder their own citizens, and referring to the free press as the enemy of the people." -

Senate Democratic Leader Charles Schumer (N.Y.) and House Minority Leader Nancy Pelosi (Calif.) in a joint statement.

Compare this with the statements of Maxine Waters, Eric holder, Hillary Clinton, Chuck Schumer, Cory Booker, Kamala Harris, Nancy Pelosi, and many other of the same breed.

Rule # 1: Accuse others of doing the things of which YOU are guilty.

49 – On the Hunt

Thought for the day Oct. 28, 2018
You believe?

There was a massacre at a Jewish synagogue Yesterday.

By a nut.

The mail Bomber is in custody.

A real nut.

The internet is advertising "Human feces map" for tourists in San Francisco.

Want to experience what the Wild, Wild west was like? Visit Southside Chicago.

Want to see Poverty in the Real? Drive the streets of Los Angeles.

Headline today: MEXICAN POLICE ALLOW MIGRANTS TO ADVANCE NORTH!

Headline tomorrow: CALAMITY NEARING TEXAS BORDER!

Headline November 6: AMERICA'S FUTURE IN THE BALANCE! VOTE!!!! How can anyone think with all this going on?

SIC 'EM DONALD!!!

Thought for the day Oct. 29, 2018
On the hunt

This man is Robert Mueller, Special Investigator, AND a real Pro of the underground Elite.

He was named such on May 17, 2017. Purpose: Investigate alleged collusion between Trump campaign and Russia.

(Hidden goal: Impeach Donald Trump) Hired 17 Democrat lawyers. Has spent millions.

Found no collusion on Trump.

Still digging.

Exposed collusion of Clinton and DNC with Russia.

Said collusion ignored.

Purpose expanded: Investigate Trump's "amateur" friends and associates.

Find dirt, any kind of dirt. Prosecute, intimidate, badger, threaten, destroy.

Mueller's past MO. Relishes job. Loves to punish.

Thrives on POWER!!!!!!!!!
SHOULD BE GONE!!!
FIRE HIM, DONALD!!!

Thought for the day Oct. 31, 2018
Halloween every day!

There is a person under that blanket and a port-a-potty in the background.

TYPHUS EPIDEMIC IN LOS ANGELES What is typhus?

(the following was copied from a news item. Not my words)

A typhus infection can cause, high fever and, in rare cases, meningitis and death. According to the L.A. health department website, it's contracted when "the feces from infected fleas

are rubbed into cuts or scrapes in the skin or rubbed into the eyes." The L.A. County Homeless Services Authority counts 2,145 people living outdoors in the skid row neighborhood. The nonprofit research organization Economic Roundtable estimates that 102,955 homeless people call L.A. county home. Andy Bales, CEO of the Union Rescue Mission, which has nearly 1,400 beds for the displaced, said the city and county governments can only do so much to alleviate a homeless problem that has sparked outbreaks of

Hepatitis A, typhus and gang violence over the skid row drug trade.

My comment: We need more illegal immigrants sleeping in the street and voting Democrat! YEAH.

SIC 'EM DONALD!!

Thought for the day Nov 2, 2018
Fools rush in where angels fear to tread.

And here I go.

Have you noticed how subdued Republicans have been?

Have you noticed how loud Democrats have been? Riots, marching in the streets, screaming like uncivilized animals, wildly criticizing President for everything he says, or does, and everything he doesn't say or do?

BJ Melton

It is my belief that Republicans and the good people of America are appalled by the vitriol and uncouth behavior of the Democrats.

(See Judge Kavanaugh)

The Democrats, through their use of 'free speech', have told the American people what low life Democrats really are. Their loud, vulgar, obscene vulgarities are meant to silence the 'free speech' of others, and it appears they have "temporarily" done so.

Here is where this fool rushes IN!

Tuesday, Nov. 6, 2018, Republicans, Independents, Libertarians, and many disgusted Democrats, will flood the polls, breaking their silence and vote for 'Freedom", not Socialism!

Then it will be

SIC 'EM DONALD!!! MAGA

Thought for the day Nov 3, 2018
Think about

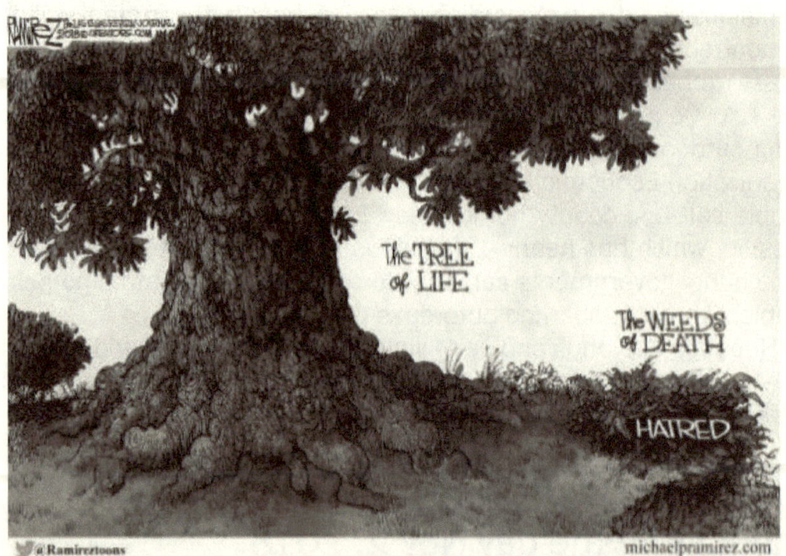

The political cartoonists are having a field day, mainly promoting hatred for something or someone. This one has a moral, a lesson for all of us. So, does this one! Self-explanatory

Thought for the day Nov. 5, 2018

Guess

Tomorrow is the BIG day. VOTE!
Everybody is playing the game:
GUESS WHAT THE COMPOSITION OF CONGRESS WILL BE AFTER TOMORROW
So, for fun, why don't we play.
My guess:
House Republicans 223 Democrats 212
Senate Republicans 53 Democrats 47

Idle Thought for the day Nov. 6, 2018

Depressing

Depressing thought any day

Be you didn't know this either.

Thought for the day Nov.6, 2018
ELECTION DAY
What will tomorrow bring?

THIS

OR THIS?

Thought for the Day Nov. 7, 2018
POST ELECTION DAY
Not a big win or loss, just a cloudy day.

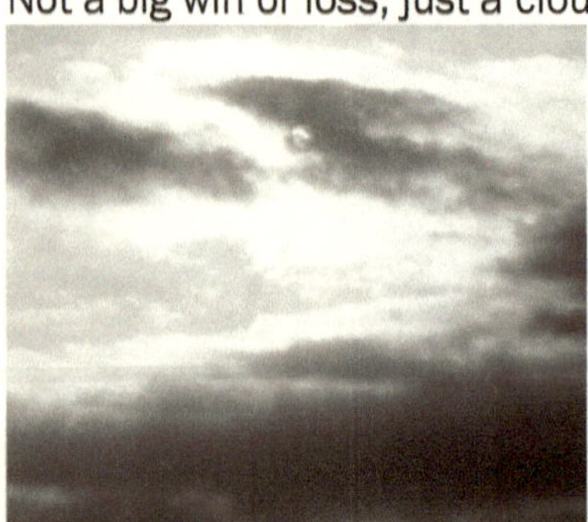

This morning when I woke up, it was a dark and gloomy day. But the fact I woke up at all, told me it will a sunny day!

Thought for the day Nov. 11, 2018
Armistice Day
Today marks the 100th anniversary of the end of World War I, a war that was billed to be "The war to end all wars".

Today, most of us know that was not true. Since 1918, we have had WW II, Korean war, and Vietnam war.

Sic 'Em Donald!

The bible tells us there will always be wars and rumors of wars. History proves this is true, with exclamation marks!!!!!!!!!!!!!!!!!!!!!!!!!
So, why do we have wars?
God created man and charged him with the responsibility to take care of His jewel, earth.
Unfortunately, but purposely it seems, he made some things good and some things bad, and he gave man the ability to think, and the option to choose.
It is the nature of most men to want freedom to live as he pleases.
Some men, by choice, are evil and want to deny you freedom.
When that freedom is violated and taken away,
Good people are willing to fight TO THE DEATH to reclaim it, AND, THEN, WE HAVE WAR!
Consequently, we have thousands, even millions, of good young people dying, while killing thousands, even millions, of bad young people, so that survivors can enjoy peace and freedom.
So..... here we are today, living in peace and freedom, thanks to millions who came before us, and paid the ultimate price. Give thanks, and pray you will NOT see the next war, whenever it comes!!!!!!!!!!
LOVE THY NEIGHBOR!

WAR IS NASTY!

Thought for the day Nov. 12, 2018
BROWARD COUNTY, FLORIDA Election Fraud?

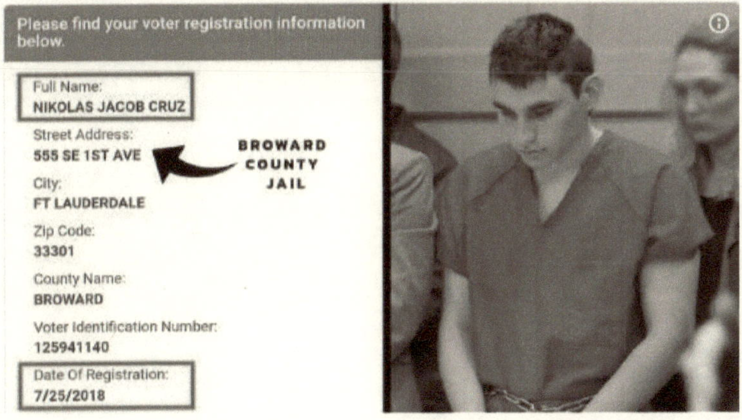

REMEMBER THIS YOUNG MAN?
His name is Nikolas Jacob Cruz.

BJ Melton

On February 16, 2018, he murdered 17 people at Parkland School. On July 25, 2018, the Democrat sheriff of Broward County, allowed individuals into his jail to register felons and other undesirables to vote.

Last week we learned Broward county can count votes, illegal votes, duplicate and triplicate votes, out-of-state votes, unregistered-to-vote votes, and, if necessary, discover thousands of uncounted votes. One precinct, with about 260 registered voters, recorded nearly 700 votes.

This is the same county that nearly bought Al Gore the Presidency in 2000. Incidentally, God's 10 Commandments are NOT posted anywhere in Broward County.

Now, don't misunderstand me, I am not saying there is fraud in Broward County.............but................

50 – Lesson in French

Thought for the day Nov. 13, 2018
Lesson in French

This is Emanuel Macron, President of France. Emanuel is 40 years old, born in 1977, 60 years after the end of WW I, 30 years after the end of WW II, and 8 years after the end of the Vietnam War.

He has never experienced war of any kind. He speaks French. He just spent November 10, 11, with President Trump, when dignitaries from around the world met in France, to remember the 100th anniversary of the end of WW I, "The war to end all wars"!

He spent time with Trump and sharply criticized him for his "Selfish" 'America First' position. Trump reminded him, that in 1918, America sacrificed 100,000 soldiers so he could speak French, not German.

To emphasize his point, Trump reminded him That in the 1940's America sacrificed several hundred thousand more soldiers, so he could speak French. He also reminded him that thousands of American soldiers, who sacrificed their lives to save France, and allow him to speak French, ARE BURIED ON FRENCH SOIL!! President Macron is wiser today than he was last week.

SIC 'EM DONALD!!!

Thought for the day Nov. 15, 2018
Problems

I woke up this morning thinking about what I could think about as my "Thought for the day"

I mulled over several things like: ......Porn lawyer Avenatti being arrested and accused of assault and battery, and I think "What's next?"

....the Florida election——the crooks recounting, and recounting votes, mixing good votes with bad votes, and adding blank votes to vote votes! Can't help but think "What's next?" ....or the Georgia election. Ditto vote count problems!

Ditto "What's next?" ....Or Yesterday, busloads of "invaders" were dropped off at the US border with Tijuana. They are running around celebrating and climbing the wall.

Now here is a really big "WHAT'S NEXT?" and I am afraid of <u>what is next</u>. ....I do not want to think about it!!

Signing off!

Thought for the day Nov. 21, 2018
Winners and Losers

The election took its toll on me, so I have been recuperating with a sabbatical. If you don't care what you say, I guess you could say "It was an interesting election". We had candidates concede, revoke their concession, then re-concede, reluctantly, again. Then demand a machine recount, and, then a hand count. There were lost ballots (conveniently), duplicate ballots, bad ballots mixed with good ballots, uncounted ballots, and voters from out-of-state.

There were happy winning candidates. There were belligerent, hateful, going to sue, and/or boycott, Losing candidates. There were winners promising to help President Trump with his America First agenda. There were winners who promised to destroy everything Donald has accomplished so far, and IMPEACH HIM!!

This is what we see. What we don't see are the well-financed Swamp critters and Shadow Guvment, continuing their plan of destruction for America. They will continue promoting hate for everything good, bringing frivolous lawsuits, and the hooded, black-suited, Antifa groups will continue riots across the country, destroying property, and defying anyone, you, me, the police, to get in their way.

AND THERE WILL BE MALICIOUS FAKE NEWS COMING AT YOU FAST AND FURIOUS, WITH JUST ONE INTENT:

Create doubt in your mind about the direction Trump is trying to take us, to make America Great Again. Question everything!!!

SIC 'EM DONALD!!!

Thought for the day Nov. 27, 2018
IMPEACHMENT?

Well before the 2016 election, Maxine Waters was calling "Impeach Trump. Impeach Trump!" She has continued her tirade ever since. Now, since the Demos will have a House majority in January, she is yelling "We got the power. We got the power."

"Now we will impeach Trump. Then, get that lying Pence!!" Think about this. Two Presidents have been impeached by the House, both

Democrats, Andrew Jackson and Bill Clinton, each was acquitted by the Senate. Nixon, a Republican, probably would have been impeached, but resigned.

Consider this scenario as of today: Trump is impeached, found guilty, leaves office. Pence becomes President. Paul Ryan becomes Vice President. Pence is impeached, found guilty, leaves office. Paul Ryan becomes President. Orin Hatch becomes Vice president. Fast forward to Jan. 10, 2019.

The scenario changes: Trump is impeached, found guilty, leaves office. Pence becomes President. Nancy Pelosi becomes Vice President. Pence is impeached, found guilty, leaves office. Nancy Pelosi becomes President. Charles Grassley becomes Vice President. Fantasy? Let's hope and pray so!!!

SIC 'EM DONALD!!!

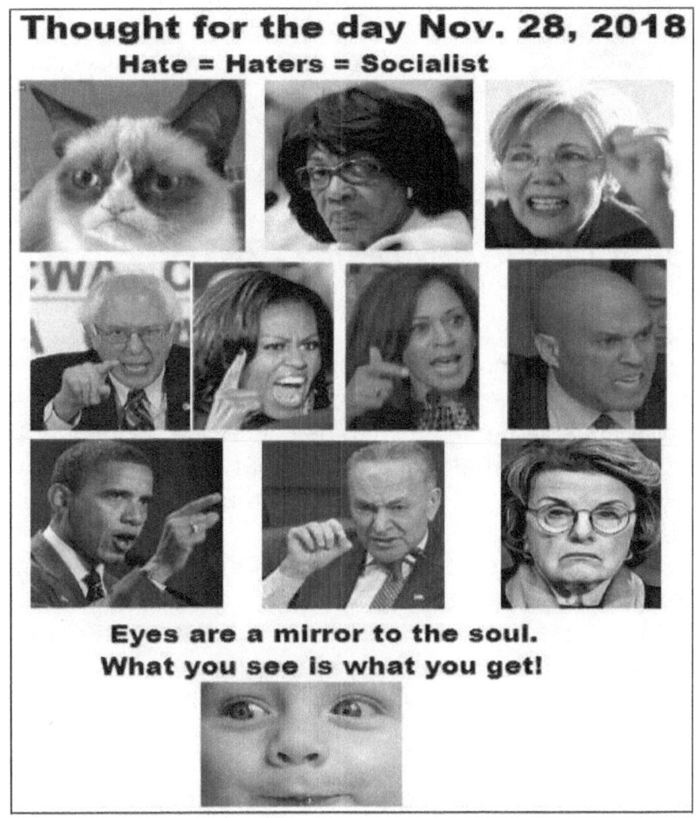

Thought for the day Nov 19, 2018
Lying

We seem to have a new fad developing. Michael Cohen, Trump's former lawyer, has admitted to lying to Congress.

To satisfy Special Counsel Robert Mueller, maybe save his hide, or get a reduced sentence, he appears to be lying about lying. (In a former world, this would be called bribery)

During the hearing with Judge Kavanaugh, lying took a front row seat, and liars started lying about lying.

Next step, I suppose, will be to lie about lying to cover lying about lying.

PS: I really like the red Christmas trees in the White House,

AND THAT'S THE TRUTH!!!

SIC 'EM DONALD!!!

Thought for the day Dec. 2, 2018
Help

You may wonder why my thoughts have been erratic.

Then, again you may have thought nothing about it.

Well, it is not because of an absence of thoughts, because there is much to think about, and much to be concerned about.

I sit here pondering about things that need fixing, and, sadly, I realize there is nothing I can do, and perhaps there is nothing any of us can do.

Socialism has taken over our schools and universities, feeding the leaders of tomorrow mush!

Socialism has taken over what was the Democrat party, which is energetically promoting free stuff for everybody.

Conservative Republicans just sit and watch.

They have no plan, no energy, to rebut what is becoming inevitable, another Valenzuela.

Consider this. Millions of legal and illegal immigrants are living here, having babies, all US citizens, all with their hand out, all voting for the Gimme Party, Socialism.

Today, there are 6000 thousand immigrants trying to invade our country, sitting in Tijuana, that are being fed, clothed, and provided medical care with money from Socialists in the USA, who say they want OPEN BORDERS!!!

Let anyone in!!!!!!!!!!!!!!!!!!!!!

The picture I have tried to paint is bad, but <u>reality</u> is much, much worse.

President Trump is trying to save us, but the hill is steep, VERY, VERY steep.

SIC 'EM DONALD!!!

Thought for the day Dec. 4, 2018
Enigmas (This one is a little stupid)

The world is full of enigmas. Here are two I find interesting.

#1. While being interrogated by Congress, Hillary replied "I can't remember" 40 (forty) times.

Most questions were simple, some of which I knew the answer. Yet, she remembered enough to write a book of 500+ pages. I guess she has 'selective' forgetting.

#2. Before being elected, President-to-be Trump <u>did</u> meet and have conversations with an 'unknown' Russian agent. (Trump later accused of 'Russian collusion'.)

COLLUDER   COLLUDED

You see, over a 2-year time span, the Russian agent ('colluder') met with the President-to-be ('colluded') several times. The 'colluded' gets investigated for 'collusion' and is hounded day and night for 2 years while trying to MAGA!! The 'colluder' goes on a Speaking Tour with 'beloved' husband, raking in the dough from the gullibles.

SIC 'EM DONALD!!!

Thought for Dec.1 to Dec. 6, 2018

Life, it seems, has been on a fast track lately.

President George H. W. Bush passed away Friday November 30.

That triggered a weeklong series of events.

That same day the G20 Summit convened in Argentina. On Saturday, President Trump had dinner with China leader Xi to discuss trade.

Sunday, the news was positive for a trade agreement.

Monday, the stock market was up. Overnight, the news soured and, Tuesday, the market tried to wipe out my little nest egg.

Market was closed Wednesday For H. W. funeral.

Today, I panicked, sold out.

But so what? All the above is completely overshadowed this week, by the celebration of the life of George H. W. Bush. I have sat in awe as the memory of his life unfolded. The precision and grace of each day's ceremony, and the words so eloquently spoken, revealed a man unknown to most people, a man who truly loved his country, his family and his friends.

Those who served in World War II are known as the Greatest Generation, and rightly so.

George H.W. was one of those. He joined the army at 18, became a fighter pilot, was shot down in the Pacific, rescued by a submarine, and flew many more missions.

He was, in man's world, a real hero.

He continued to serve our country in different ways, including being Reagan's Vice President for 8 years, and President for 4 years.

In the past 5 days, our nation has bade farewell, with pomp and pageantry, to a man best remembered as a "kinder and gentler" leader who accomplished much. Severely castigated in life, he has now been venerated in death. As one speaker said, "No occupant of the Oval Office was more courageous, more principled and more honorable than George Herbert Walker Bush."

He may, perhaps, be America's last great soldier-statesman!!

In death, he has finally been accorded the role of TRUE HERO.

Thought for the day Dec. 7, 2018
President George H.W. Bush

Today is December 7, a special day for many Americans.

But for millions of Americans, it is just TGIF day. 77 years ago, it was a peaceful sleepy Sunday morning in in Hawaii. At 7:55 AM, bombs started raining on Pearl Harbor.

It was a surprise aerial attack by the Japanese. And it was unimaginable chaos. 2403 soldiers and civilians were killed, over 1200 wounded.

They sank 8 United States battle ships, 3 destroyers, 3 cruisers, mine layer, and an anti-aircraft training ship.

They also took out 188 fighter planes.
Suddenly, we were at war, not a war of our choosing,
BUT A WAR WE HAD TO FINISH, AND FINISH IT WE DID.

It was a terrible war. The price paid for victory was astronomical, 111, 606 killed or missing, 253,000 wounded, 21,580 Prisoners of War. A friend of mine (2 years older), whose father cut my hair, was caught, and survived the Bataan Death March.

There were heroes, many, many heroes. One such hero, President George H. W. Bush was laid to rest yesterday, Dec. 6, at Texas A&M in a grave by his beloved wife, Barbara. H.W. joined the navy on his 18th birthday and became the youngest fighter pilot in the war. He flew 58 missions in the Pacific.

Was shot down one time and was fortunate to be rescued. His entire life was spent serving America culminating in being elected President in 1888.

If you were born after 1935, you cannot have any personal memory of this event, only what you have been told. Your freedom has been bought with a dear price, AND YOU DON'T HAVE TO SPEAK JAPANESE!!

Thought for the day Dec. 9, 2018

Yesterday, I watched the annual Army-Navy football game. In the stands were thousands of our finest young people, Cadets (Black Knights) and Midshipman, male and female, yelling for their team. They were dressed in uniform. there were no beards, or long hair, except for females. They stood at attention for the anthem, NO KNEELING OR FIST IN THE AIR.

Made me proud!!!

When the players ran on the field many were carrying miniature stars and stripes.

Our President was marched to midfield and performed the coin toss, then the crowd erupted in a frenzy as he shook hands with the captains of each team. He sat on the Navy side in the first half, then move to Army side for 2nd half.

As the game progressed, it was obvious the two teams were enemies (but just for the day). Blocking, tackling, and running was intense.

Sometime in the 3rd quarter, I sensed something strange.

BJ Melton

Only one or two penalties had been called. I thought to myself "Why"? It has to be just one thing- DISCIPLINE!

They are taught 'control' and 'discipline' and they carry it with them in life and to the football field.

Curious, I looked up their record when the game was over. For the record, for the season Navy was #1 for fewest penalties, and Army was #4.

Contrast the Dallas Cowboys, who have minimal discipline. One player today had two holding penalties that killed one drive, and a third one, which stopped another one.

They won today with PURE DUMB luck.

SIC 'EM DONALD!!!

51 – Army – Navy Game

Thought for the day Dec. 10, 2018
THE PRAYER

As I told you Yesterday, the Army-Navy game was something special to me.

But nothing was more touching, or made me more thankful,

than the opening prayer. If you are an American, the prayer,

in reality, says to you... "You can read this because......."

Chaplain Col. Matthew Pawlikowski of the United States Military Academy

at West Point, started his invocation Saturday with his compelling reason

for praying before a football game.

"God of Wonders, some wonder why we pray for a football game. So,

I tell them, in this game, every player on the field is willing to die

for every person watching, and there is no greater love than to

lay down one's life for what's truly good. And so, God,

I do pray for these players, on this field, and all the good they represent,

and their fellow cadets and midshipmen, soldiers, sailors, Marines,

firefighters, first responders, police, and countless others who lay down their lives

daily in our defense," he continued.

"Because in your eyes, Oh God, it is not the critic who counts,

but those who actually step into the arena."

Amen

Thought for the day Dec. 12, 2018
Making soup
Yesterday, December 11, 2018 was a historic day!

Pelosi, Schumer, Pence, and President Trump, met in the White House, on live TV, to discuss the future of America.

Pelosi said, "I thought we were coming here to have a private conversation, and now, you are showing us to the world".

"It is called 'Transparency', Nancy."

Trump needs $5 billion to build a wall in critical locations. Pelosi and Schumer are offering 'crumbs', like $1.6 billion, with strings attached.

Reason? The want an Open Border. NO WALL.

Let them all come in!!! The good, bad, and ugly!

Reminds me of potato soup my mother made.

You want to know how many people a pot would feed?

Need more soup? Just add water.

Now visualize the FUTURE of AMERICA.

SIC 'EM DONALD!!

Thought for the day Dec. 13, 2018
"Come let us reason together"
This morning when I got up, I followed my usual routine, start the coffee pot, get paper in the front yard- But, Whoa! My front door was open. I always close it at night. Well, I am old, so maybe I forgot. I get my paper and a cup of coffee and head for the north bathroom to contemplate things going on in the world.

Suddenly, I hear a baby crying. It is coming from the front bedroom.

I look in the bedroom and I am shocked speechless.

Sic 'Em Donald!

There is a man and woman and a newborn baby, born during the night. Turns out they are Mexicans from Honduras, named Juan and Maria, but baby has not been named yet. Then to my surprise, in walks a Mexican boy, about 8 years old, and a girl I guessed to be about 10. I learn they are here illegally, except for the baby. The baby is an American citizen. They have moved into my house and plan to stay.

Their clothes, what they have, are already hanging in the closet. Juan asks for towels and soap to bath, for it has been a long, difficult journey. I am becoming more flabbergasted by the minute. I know I should call the police, but they seem like such nice, well deserving people. And there is the baby. I had to think about the baby, after all, it is an American citizen.

While they were bathing, I sat down in my easy chair and began to think.

How did I get in this mess? What should I do? Throw them out in the street?

Call the police and have them put in Jail? And there's the baby.

What about the baby? This is really getting complicated!

After they had bathed, they brought me their dirty clothes and asked me to wash them. And they were hungry. Juan said "NO EAT. 5 Days"

So, I fried 2 pounds of bacon and scrambled 18 eggs, saying to myself all along

"What am I doing? I must be crazy!"

After eating their fill, Juan says "U have nice place. We happy here. Think we stay". That's it! Juan, you and Maria sit down. Let us reason together. But Juan say "No reason. We like free housing, free food. We stay. Oh, get doctor free medical care for American citizen baby." Then you say this is a fantasy story. It is and it isn't.

This kind of thing has been happening all over America for years. Today we have over 11 million illegals living here, and an estimated 800,000 Dreamers, illegals brought here as children by their illegal parents.

They like it here. They want to stay. Should illegals be returned to their homeland? "Come let us reason together".

SIC 'EM DONALD! MAGA!!!

Thought for the day Dec. 18, 2018

Santa Claus

I am looking forward to a great Christmas!

However, I heard some sad news yesterday. Some people want to change Santa Claus, one of my very favorite people!

They want to change him from a smiling, Ho Ho Ho good fellow, to someone who is slimmed down, maybe wearing blue jeans, (with holes, of course), sneakers, a no tuck shirt, whiskers (not a beautiful white beard), and multi-colored hair.

Drones will replace Rudolph and the sleigh.

Crummy deal.

I miss the real Santa already. I don't even know his mailing address, so I can't write to him.

Thought for the day Dec. 20, 2018
Sic 'em Donald!!!

The last two years, for President Trump, and for America, has been, as he says, INCREDIBLE!

Much has been accomplished, some with historical significance.

Much remains to be done.

Rino Paul Ryan, Speaker of the house, with a Republican majority of 236-197, has failed Trump and America miserably!!

Under his 'leadership, the House has failed to:

-control deficit spending,

-defund Planned Parenthood,

-repeal Obamacare

-fund the Border Wall,

-or strengthen Immigration laws,

-or do much of anything Republicans promised voters. On the plus side, we got the tax cut (not Ryan's fault), and two Supreme Court Judges, thanks to the Senate. It has been an uphill climb for Donald, and Rino Ryan has been his worst enemy. When Trump announced his candidacy in 2015, Ryan did everything he could to prevent Trump from getting the nomination. And since Trump won, he has undermined him at every chance, trying to destroy his Presidency. He aspired to be President, and Trump's success has turned him into bitter, spiteful person. Now, come January 3, 2019, with Pelosi as Speaker, we have a new game.

What will the future bring?

SIC 'EM DONALD!!!

Christmas Day December 25, 2018
This will be the last page of my new book
SIC 'EM DONALD!

As a present, I will leave you with question to ponder on:

ARE YOU GLAD YOUR MOTHER WAS PRO-LIFE?

This is all for now

Thanks for reading my book.

About the Author

My name is Buster Jack Melton. It is not a name I would have chosen if I had had a choice.

So, in later life, I chose to be called just BJ.

I was born October 10, 1925 and have survived to the overly ripe age of 93. At age 16, I graduated from High School and entered Texas Tech University. At age 18, I joined the Navy and served for 20 months during World War II. Honorably discharged in 1946, I returned to Tech and graduated in 1947 with a degree in Electrical Engineering.

Three jobs later, I was hired by Texas Power & Light Company in 1953, from which I retired 34 years later. My job, among other things, required writing many technical papers and letters. As a result, I developed a strong desire to write, almost every day, recording my thoughts, ideas, memories, along with just plain nonsense!!

When General Eisenhower became President, I became interested in politics, especially our Federal Government. That interest has intensified in the last 30 years, as the country I remember during my youth, is changing-and not for the better! The presidencies of Clinton, Bush, and Obama began to accelerate My America more and more toward Progressive Socialism which, to me, is an abomination. It became obvious, at least to me, that the heir apparent to Obama would continue this trend. When Donald announced his candidacy for President, he talked like I talk, and thought like I think. Immediately, my writings turned to promoting Trump for President.

My first book, "My America Is Back, Thoughts of a Patriot," covered the Period from June 15, 2015, through July 31, 2017. This book, "Sic 'Em Donald!!", is a sequel and continues my thoughts from August 2017 through December 30, 2018.

I cannot hide my obvious bias toward my President Trump, nor do I want to. If you feel offended by what I have written, I hope you will just thoughtfully dwell on the right or wrong of what I say.

Sadly, America today is filled with hate and is destroying the Light on the Hill.

Remember this..................... HATRED ONLY DESTROYS THE VESSELS THAT CARRY IT

B J Melton